OUTRAGED

DEAR _____

SO NICE TO MEET YOU / THE
PERSON WHO GOT THIS BOOK FOR
YOU!
    I HOPE YOU LOVE THE BOOK.

    KINDEST REGARDS

(BEN HENRY - AUTHOR!)

PAUL HENRY

OUTRAGED

RANDOM HOUSE
NEW ZEALAND

NOTE:
THE VIEWS EXPRESSED IN THIS BOOK ARE NOT NECESSARILY THOSE OF RANDOM HOUSE... OK!.

A RANDOM HOUSE BOOK published by Random House New Zealand
18 Poland Road, Glenfield, Auckland, New Zealand

For more information about our titles go to www.randomhouse.co.nz

A catalogue record for this book is available from the National Library of New Zealand
Random House New Zealand is part of the Random House Group
New York   London   Sydney   Auckland   Delhi   Johannesburg

First published 2013, reprinted 2013, 2014.
© 2013 Paul Henry

The moral rights of the author have been asserted

ISBN 978 1 77553 521 8
eISBN 978 1 77553 522 5

Literary assistant: Linzi Dryburgh
Design: Megan van Staden and Paul Henry
Front cover painting: Pricasso
Cover photographs and studio portrait images of Paul Henry: Jane Ussher
Image on page 51: Boris Ryzhkov/Photos.com

Printed in New Zealand by Printlink

ILLUSTRATOR

I have been very fortunate to be able to secure the services once again of one of New Zealand's pre-eminent illustrators.

Olive Mary Christine Hopes has a comparatively short but illustrious history as a literary illustrator. In fact all the projects she has worked on to date have become bestsellers.

As she ages (and she is now very old indeed), her masterpieces, far from deteriorating in technique, have taken on more of a Dali-esque quality. This is largely due to failing eyesight, a crumbling mind, arthritis and a potpourri of medication.

Perhaps the most important quality Olive displays is that of a loving mother. She is my mother; I am very proud of her. And I love her dearly.

COVER ARTIST

Performance artist Pricasso has stunned audiences all over the world with his creations. Pricasso is thought to be the only professional artist to exclusively paint with his penis. Both flaccid and erect, Pricasso can fashion a likeness in a very short time. Artists around the globe have expressed their amazement at his ability to capture the essence of a face with only a few strokes of his tool. Audiences have just expressed their amazement!

NOTE:

Backgrounds are often painted with Pricasso's bare butt cheeks in order to reduce over-use of his penis.

DEDICATION

To a significantly sized group of people of whom I am blissfully aware: those who are outraged by me. I dedicate this book to you in the hope that:

1. You have paid full retail price for it, and

2. I continue to outrage, offend and appal you.

The only shame is that you are unaware of the extent to which you are undeserving of my talents. May your numbers grow.

DISCLAIMER

Over the years, on numerous occasions people have expressed their surprise that I seem to have an opinion on everything. When people say to me, 'What do you think about this?', I am never short of an opinion, regardless of whether or not I care particularly about what it is the person is referring to. This is because I am both intelligent and broad of vision. I would, for example, never respond with 'I don't care', 'I'm not sure', 'I don't know' or 'I haven't thought about it enough to have made up my mind'. There are many things about which I care little or nothing, but I still have an opinion on them. For instance, should homosexuals be allowed to marry? I actually don't care, but my opinion is 'No, they shouldn't'. There will be more on this later, in the chapter covering why I am outraged by homosexuals.

The purpose of this disclaimer is to point out that everything contained in the pages of this book represents my personal opinion on a range of subjects, at this particular point in time. There is *no* point of contention. These *are* my views. End of story.

Luckily, I am easily outraged. While the world is essentially paradise, and in New Zealand we are particularly lucky to experience paradise acutely, nonetheless it is full of shits, arseholes, mindless bureaucracy and petty prejudices. This is grist to my mill, because unlike so many people I am not shy of expressing my opinions and calling things for what they are. This is because I actually don't care what people think of me. And I am not at all sure why that is. My mother, whose mind is increasingly letting her down, is a delightful woman whom I love dearly. But like many, particularly of her generation, she feels inferior, not worthy and frightened of authority, and has a desire and concern to be liked and accepted. Why none of that is important to me is quite frankly beyond me. It must just be that I am so confident I am both *right* and *good*.

I recall once sitting in a bombed-out café in a destroyed village, somewhere in Croatia, with a beautiful girl in her early twenties. This was her home, the only home she had ever known; and this was her war, hers through birth. Most of her family, her friends and all of her freedoms were gone. Her past destroyed, her future hopes and dreams shattered, or at the very least changed forever.

You might well be wondering where I am going with this — the book is an emotional rollercoaster.

The thing is, I was talking to this girl about her extraordinary situation. 'What,' I said to her, 'is the very worst thing about your circumstances?' And in the midst of this desolation she told me that by far the worst thing in her life was her inability to openly say how she felt. To speak her mind. To tell her truth. She told me that the sickest societies must surely be those where people are condemned or killed for saying how they feel.

HOUSEKEEPING

Since everything in life — thanks largely to OSH or its equivalent — seems to start with someone pointing out the location of the toilets, the exits and giving some half-arsed direction with regard to procedures in the unlikely event that an alarm sounds, I have decided to start this book with a little housekeeping.

As the very existence of OSH or its equivalent is one of the many things that outrage me, I won't do them the service of pointing out the obvious. Such as what to do in the event of a paper cut, sore or tired eyes as the result of lengthy reading in poor light, or the

dangers of becoming engrossed in my book while operating heavy machinery. Let's face it, like the locations of the exits, if you can't work this out for yourself then you are wasting both your time and mine, in that you are unlikely to comprehend anything that follows.

However, in the unlikely event that you drop this book in the dark, lighting will appear to guide you to its whereabouts. Please follow the instructions of the voice inside your head, which I accept has led you astray on many occasions over the years.

So, while this book contains many pages that are consecutively numbered, it is not essential that the following chapters be read in any particular order. You can, for instance, read the book from the back to the front, more or less, (particularly if you are of Asian extraction) and the end result will be about the same.

While what's in this book is damned entertaining, you should be prepared to be frustrated and even at times outraged yourself by some of my opinions. Now *that's* value for money!

While I find the sporadic changing of font sizes and styles and the odd placement of blank sections damned frustrating, you will notice

I **have** utilised these **techniques** at **times.** Partly to pad it out, partly to give you the satisfaction of thinking you read faster than you really do, but mostly because it is my book and I have chosen to.

Finally, I am not a particularly litigious person and I will not tolerate legal advances from those who are. If there is something in this book that offends you to the point that you choose to take it further, good luck to you; I will have no part of it.

CONTENTS

QUEUING FOR THE CARRY-ON LUGGAGE X-RAY MACHINE AT AIRPORTS

I am regarded by many as arrogant, and while this is a wholly incomplete description of my persona, it is not wholly inaccurate. I am a very complex individual. And, yes, arrogance is a trait I rightfully display at times. There is, though, a form of arrogance I never display. It is an arrogance I condemn completely. It manifests in individuals who are so self-obsessed that they are blind to others. These people feature heavily in many chapters in this book. Irrespective of how deserving or otherwise, rich or poor, wholesome or corrupt you are, the queue for the luggage scanner at airports is the great leveller. The élite passengers such as myself, who up to this point have been segregated by one of the last wonderful remnants of a legal class system, now mix uncomfortably with the riff-raff just before, together, we embark on the indignity of having our prized possessions irradiated.

It is here that these supremely arrogant morons are at their most harmful. Why, while they have waited in the queue, did they not remove their laptops from their rucksacks? Why did they not sip the last of their water from their stupid sipping bottles? And what made them think that they were so special that they could get a litre bottle of breast milk onto a plane to so-say 'feed a child'? They cluster at the entrance to the x-ray machine pulling Christ only knows what out of their pockets, rifling through their belongings and saying things like, 'Well, where am I going to get a little plastic bag now?' Back and forth they go, to the annoying tune of the electronic warning as yet another metal object is found about their person. All the while holding me up. Suited businesspeople travelling together are often completely oblivious to the queue they are in, let alone the people they are queuing with. They are engaged in life-changing conversations about some bloody computer thing or stupid damn product, when, ALL OF A SUDDEN, 'Ooh, we're at the x-ray machine! It's time to toy with the idea of removing from our luggage the myriad electronic devices we have and decanting our Old Spice!'

I am within sniffing distance of the Air New Zealand lounge. I can almost taste the wine and the gluten-free treats they have prepared for me. I can't access any of this, though, until these people, for whom air travel seems to come as something of a last-minute shock, get out of my way. Like voting, there should be some kind of simply administered test to ascertain whether or not someone is too stupid to fly. That would surely cull the dead wood from the queue for the carry-on luggage x-ray machine.

There are many jobs I couldn't possibly imagine being able to tolerate; working on one of these x-ray machines would be one of them. How these people avoid the urge to stab to death these mindless individuals, I have no idea.

QUESTION: Why can't I take this large bottle of water on this plane? It's only a bottle of water . . .
ANSWER: *Six abrupt, forceful lunges at the chest with confiscated nail scissors.*

QUESTION: Do I need to take my laptop out of my rucksack?
ANSWER: *Six abrupt face blows with the back of a Compaq Presario.*

Now this kind of theatre would be worth waiting in line for.

NOTE:

If you recognise yourself by the behaviour described, you could be thinking: 'Who the hell does Henry think he is? He can just wait in line for me to bugger around as much as I like.' Do you see how arrogant you are?

Fix yourself. Or don't travel.

PAUL HENRY

Despite being aware of a small selection of less-than-optimal personal traits, coupled with an almost insignificant number of partial inadequacies, I consider myself to be perfect. If, though, I were pinned to muddy ground next to a rising freshwater tide occupied by piranhas and forced to acknowledge something about myself that should outrage me, it would be this: my life has been compromised by my inability to apply myself to any task for any significant length of time. In short, I can't knuckle down.

That's why I have no career. It has just been a series of jobs. I have witnessed colleagues crawl over upturned bottle-tops to attend the opening of another tedious show or go to another dreadful celebrity party only because it might be good for their career. *Might*. I would rather not have a job at all than spend any time talking to dull people who are only there themselves to advance their positions.

On numerous occasions I have placed significant obstacles in the way of people trying to offer me, or persuade me to do, things that others would die for the opportunity to do.

Writing this book alone requires all my concentration and a bevy of souls to wrestle me to a computer or iPad. It's not that I don't want to do it. Well, it sort of is. It's mostly, though, that I am quite happy to put things off and risk never doing them. I have just done so much already. My enthusiasm for ticking boxes has waned to an imperceptible trickle. I can only imagine how successful I might have been had I been different. That's if I could be bothered to imagine it. So, as the piranhas lacerated my private parts I would reluctantly confess to outrage at my comparative apathy to my own advancement.

FOOTNOTE:

A special thank you to all those who turned up to my last book launch, of *What Was I Thinking*, in 2011. To be honest, it was a bit of fun. I am sure no careers were advanced, although I did catch at least two people pitching book ideas to my publisher . . . Opportunistic bastards.

SKYCITY

The debate surrounding the Auckland Convention Centre and SkyCity's 'deal with the government' highlights the huge void between what Helen Clark would refer to as the 'wreckers and haters' and the reasonable people who want to advance New Zealand as a great place to live, work and visit.

Now, I have an association with SkyCity. It is an association I am proud of. Why? Because SkyCity is an enterprise that represents quality, exceptional business practice, and continual advancement for our country. One of the biggest employers, ratepayers and taxpayers in the country, they are also progressive. Building and running the best restaurants, function centres, hotels and — yes — gambling facilities.

No one else came up with a convention centre plan that came close to that of SkyCity's, but, because the company required financial incentive to realise it, the wowsers were out in force. The socialists, the greenies and the feral sector generally condemned the deal based on the fact that it was not perfect. After all, it is true that some stupid people who can't regulate their own lives will be harmed by the introduction of more pokie machines. Just like some will eat themselves into *The Guinness Book of World Records* because of the advancement of McDonald's evil plan! These are real problems and are being addressed by society and by SkyCity. Sadly, these moral crusaders, most of whom are sucking on the public tit, 'queer the pitch' by misrepresenting the negatives and completely overlooking the positives. One of the things they dislike most about SkyCity is its persistent desire to make a profit. Those bastards at SkyCity, who do they think they are? They should run on the same basis as the many, many charities they support. Donation.

SKY
Tower

24

It is shameful how the naysayers — many of whom are politicians — misrepresent situations to further their own agendas. Sadly, many of these people know nothing about making money or even the need to make money. They know only how to spend other people's money. The wowsers need to recognise that some must be permitted to profit in order to top up the coffers from which they spend.

SUPPLEMENTARY:

The luxury suites at the top of the SkyCity Hotel are designed for the very high-rollers from mostly Asia, and are a model of how the ideal small country would run. Let's go offshore and import rich people for a few days to deposit large quantities of foreign currency in New Zealand, and in doing so employ New Zealanders. Let's get these high-rollers to bring with them friends and family who will visit retail and tourist facilities, showering the land with their largesse.

What did the wowsers say when SkyCity opened this top-end operation? They complained that these rich people from other lands might be given preferential treatment at the border! Yes, they would rather the high-rollers and their entourages did not come. Let's face it, they would rather they did not exist at all. Well, if facilities like this were not here, the high-rollers would not come. They would still exist, but they would be depositing their wealth in other lands just as they did before this 'rich wing' was opened.

The best thing, though, about this wonderland of opulence high above the mindless deliberations of the lefty 'wreckers and haters' (thank you, Helen!) is that, if you are ever lucky enough to get there, you can be sure of one thing — you will never bump into any of them!

CELEBRITY ENDORSEMENTS

There is nothing wrong with celebrity endorsements so long as you, as a celebrity, follow a few simple rules.

First, would you or did you recommend this service or product to friends and family prior to your involvement, and were you using it, or would you have used it if you had been aware? Are you genuinely enthusiastic about it, trusting it and trusting in it?

Secondly, have you done due diligence on it, if necessary? It is one thing to be cavalier with your own money, but you must not be cavalier with the money of others.

Thirdly, you must be completely up-front about your endorsement. If you shy away from it at any time, it indicates you are not proud to be associated with the service or product, which just makes you a shabby opportunist who can't be trusted. A shallow, money-grabbing little shit.

A celebrity endorsement has to become part of the celebrity's way of life, to an extent.

You must also recognise what is and what is not a celebrity endorsement. Rachel Hunter was just advertising Trumpet, as I was just advertising Snickers. Now I would not be involved in an advertisement for anything I did not like and trust, and I have been involved with very few advertisements, but they are just ads, not endorsements. (Having said this, I do accept that in a sense any association is a partial endorsement, which is why celebrities are always in demand for adverts.) Rachel's Pantene involvement, though, is a perfect example of a long, successful endorsement association, and one which has even become inter-generational with her daughter getting involved. The current Jennifer Aniston skin cream thing is another good example. She tried so many creams that let her down on the life journey she took to find this one. Just like Katy Perry, whose face must have been a nightmare to control until she found what's-its-name!

Richard Long's advertising involvement with the investment company Hanover Finance turned into the ultimate nightmare. His association with the company definitely fell into the endorsement category, as it lasted so long and banked on his perceived trustworthiness as a news presenter. What a diabolical cluster-fuck for Long. I think I felt sorry for him at the time the whole thing went arse-up. He was the perfect fit for them. Turns out they did not deserve him. All part of life's rich tapestry.

The celebrity endorsement that makes my blood boil is one that I personally became intertwined in as a victim. I was hunting down a reasonably priced can-opener in The Warehouse when I started to tingle at the sight of a range of helpful kitchen devices brandishing the image of a famous celebrity cook. It featured her smiling, trustworthy and — from a culinary perspective — expert image. You can just picture my level of shopper's arousal when I saw that her excellent, personally endorsed range included a can-opener for only a few dollars. 'I'll have that!' I eagerly exclaimed, and bought it without a second thought. After all, she had done the thinking for me. I rushed home where a can was waiting to be opened.

What a useless price of crap. It opened half a can before I threw it in the bin. Price per use? About $2.75. Most expensive price-per-use can-opener I'll ever buy. I thought, 'How is it possible that her pudgy little fingers grasped that crappy object, held it to the rim of a can, and she thought, 'How wonderful! I'll have a piece of that!' What a truly ghastly chapter in my life.

I am not going to mention the Briscoes lady at all. She falls into a whole different category: people who are celebrities because of a long involvement with an organisation. They don't need to follow any rules, and need only be concerned, like most people doing a job, with the pay cheque. Simple. There, not going to mention her at all then!

PERSONAL ENDORSEMENTS:

I am very proud to have a small association with two companies. They are both organisations that I was enthusiastic about prior to my involvement with them. Both SkyCity and Air New Zealand are excellent corporate assets to our country, providing world-class services.

MUSIC ON NEW ZEALAND PUBLIC RADIO

Some of the talk on National Radio is nothing short of unbridled wankery. Trumped-up quasi-academic discussions of no importance and no interest, which in the real world would not pass muster. But New Zealand public radio is not about the real world. And I get that. Unlike the complete waste of money spent on the Concert Programme — that is what it was called the last time I twisted my Bakelite knob too far left: shut it down now! — I concede there is reason to invest a comparatively small amount of our money in public radio. But the music they play is shit.

Okay, so a bit of jazz . . . No, not even that! What was I thinking? Have the socialist academic glitterati never heard of the iPod? I don't need to be subjected to ethnic flute-playing, moaning, chanting or tribal ankle-bells clinking on. And I certainly don't need to be paying for it.

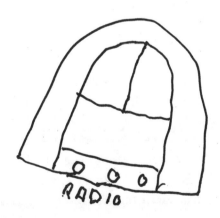

RADIO

In response to this, the probably lesbian and certainly Labour-voting programmer would say, 'It's an opportunity to hear things that would otherwise not be played.' Yes, it is. And for very good reason: it's crap!

The tiny group who like it can buy it and listen to it all the time. They are not listening to National Radio anyway. They are at home with their myriad of children, fixing their taxi on the front lawn, and preparing a feast for some festival I have never heard of and never want to. And when they are at the festival, National Radio will probably be broadcasting it. The difference between National Radio and public access radio is paper-thin!

NOTE:

Do not be fooled. Just because there are long pauses and thoughtful tones, it is not necessarily quality. Just like on the marae, the clearing of throats and coughing does not in itself denote wisdom. It could just be asthma.

ANECDOTE:

Some years ago I found myself driving through a forest with no signal to keep me company but that of National Radio. It was early afternoon, and a small clan of travelling minstrels were recounting their seemingly endless experiences and musing on their spiritual inspirations. For an hour. Jesus Christ, it was appalling radio. As a broadcaster I was transfixed by its diabolical production values and worthless content. For me it was spectacularly entertaining, but I knew that had I turned in a programme only twice as good when I was a cadet, years earlier, it would have been instantly rejected for the dross it was.

INSTRUCTION TO GOVERNMENT:

Immediately cut funding to the Concert Programme, or whatever it's called, and divest the assets. Rid us of the expense and unbridled wankery, and save us from funding a job-creation scheme for élitist socialists. The audience of nine can easily download classical entertainment on their i-machines! Let them pay for that, as is their democratic right, and stop forcing the rest of us to pay for this lunacy.

So what to do with the comparatively small number of millions of dollars you are now saving? Give it to the élitist wankers at the NZSO. They can start an NZISO with the extra funding. This New Zealand Inspirational Symphony Orchestra (working title only) will act as a feeder to the NZSO, and so build its capacity. Its main purpose is to continuously travel New Zealand, expanding the minds and broadening the vision of young New Zealanders through classical music, in every nook and cranny of paradise. A much better reach of this kind of culture than the Concert Programme could ever hope to achieve.

PLASTIC SHOPPING BAGS

Plastic shopping bags are a convenience product. They are the creation of a consumer society, not of the Devil. They are fantastic. Not just for the logistics of their prime design, but for their reuse potential. Rubbish bags, crocheted into hats, or simply ironed together to make original art or toilet-roll holders —

plastic shopping bags are **brilliant.**

Some will tell you that they are killing whales. Absolute shite! Show me one whale cadaver full of shopping bags. You can't. I propose that not one whale in the history of the globe has been so much as inconvenienced by a plastic shopping bag. However, *I* have been inconvenienced many times by the lack of one. On the grounds that restricting the availability of these bags will save the planet, retailers charge for them. Bastards and cowards. What do these retailers do with all the 10 cents collected? Give it to the multinational organisation Greenpeace? Laugh all the way to the bank, more like it, as half their customers drop the multitude of objects they are trying to juggle in the car park, in an effort to avoid the tax.

As for the environment — I can't believe I am bothering with this line of argument! — let's buy potentially-more-harmful bin-liners. God, let's just buy them anyway and burn them on the lawn!

Bunnings don't charge for plastic bags. They just don't have them. How much do they make selling bin-liners, I wonder? ('Excuse me, sir, can I help you pick up all your bolts and washers?' 'No — but you can give me a fuck'n bag to put them in!')

The Warehouse — where everyone gets a bargain that they

can fumble and drop next to their car — I have been told have considered backtracking on the policy like some others. (Was it some New World supermarkets who have gone back to providing a logistics service, and now once again give you a bag?) Probably because, as we all know, the threat to the planet has now passed! What a bunch of wowsers!

In the Bay area of San Francisco all of the retailers have decided to band together and charge 10 cents for a bag. I have juggled yoghurt, chocolate, cans of drink, inexpensive Merlot and postcards several blocks from Walgreens to my hotel to avoid this evil and stupid tax. Brought about by damned greenies and a society too frightened to say, 'Fuck off, you tiresome, good-for-nothing hippies. This is our planet, and we will do what we fuck'n well like with it.'

SUPPLEMENTARY FACT:

In the Bay area, Victoria's Secret charge for a bag but will still wrap your girlfriend's panties in enough complimentary tissue paper to smother a small child. They will then shroud it in ribbon. To be fair, it is the Bay area — they are probably your boyfriend's panties!

NOTE FOR RETAILERS:

With the exception of Pak'nSave, who have established a *quid pro quo* with their customers, don't bow to extremists. You are not saving the globe; you are only reticulating bits and bobs.

The following is my (I mean you now!) list of businesses I will never patronise again because they bow to the nonsense of hippies rather than value their customers.

34

'MY LIST OF PLASTIC BAG
TIGHTWADS'

NAME:

35

TAKING SNAPS

There was a time when we would all laugh at Japanese tourists. They never truly experienced anything first-hand. As soon as they got close to seeing something interesting, they would whip out their cameras and view it through a lens, then they would grab a relative and thrust them in the way of the interesting sight, just to prove later that they were also there not looking at whatever it was. We didn't know why the Japanese did this, or if they ever actually sat around looking at their snaps. I dare say if a group of them ever did congregate to view snaps, someone would have taken a picture of it.

Well, it turns out the only difference then between them and the rest of the planet was that they could afford the cost of developing! Now taking pictures is free, and everyone looks at the world through a lens or, worse, the bloody screen on an iPad. Bad enough that so much time is spent in front of television, but now, on the odd occasion you do put yourself in the position of actually living, you film it. Whoever looks back at these things anyway?

Everything gets posted on the Facebook machine or tweeted or Pinterested or Instagrammed. Just fuck'n look at it. Be there for your own sake, not for the greater good of a group of people who are much more interested in themselves than you.

TIP FOR LIVING:

Don't let dinner get cold as you position it in the best possible light to photograph it and post it. It's food, for Christ's sake — eat it.

Camra

ANECDOTE:

O n Australia Day, I had positioned myself with many thousands of others in Sydney's Darling Harbour to view the fireworks. (God, Australians love pyrotechnics.) At the first hint of a sparkle, up came the crowd's hands — a sea of phones, cameras and tablets. Photographing and filming life as it

slipped away. All these fools had gone to some trouble to get there, and now they were missing the wonder of being there. A stupid man in front of me put his son down from the vantage point on his shoulders so he could film the damn thing on his iPad. And until I told him to shift, I was actually watching the event on his screen. People are such twats.

If you do this, if this is you, rethink your priorities. You won't be given another chance to make up for wasting your life taking snaps.

PHOTO OF FIREWORKS DISPLAY
TAKEN BY MORON IN CROWD!

38

BAD TV

You will have heard people say, and marketing tell you, things like 'Life's too short to drink cheap wine / eat bad burgers / drive shit cars . . .' While this is true, it is idealistic and often, for many, unreasonable. It is also not the end of the world to drink inexpensive wine. Believe you me, many a good night has come off the back of cheap wine. A bad burger will still fill you up, and a shit car could easily deliver you in one piece to your destination.

Bad TV, on the other hand, does not reward you. It requires a commitment from you of the same amount of time as good TV, but sometimes unknowingly robs you of the will to live. Like infomercials, it cunningly plays with your mind to hook you, hold you and force you to invest.

It used to be people with desperately dull or boring lives who would sit in their huts watching richer lives. Broadening their vision with stories of adventure. Documentaries on far-flung places. Nature programmes. Programmes about pygmies (I have had a bit to do with pygmies over the years: get them drunk at your peril — very unpredictable little people in the wild!) or even lifestyles of the rich and famous.

Now people invest their precious time watching programmes on the lives of people more boring and uninteresting than themselves. **Jesus Christ,** how stupid. These programmes are designed to capture you and hold you for no reward at all.

Derrick and June have outgrown their bedsit in Durham, and, with the birth of their next set of twins only two months away, need desperately to find a bigger home. But they have been looking for over a year and have found nothing they can agree on. This is a tough one, Kirsty.

The truth is this: Derrick and June are about to suck the life blood out of you. Just as they have already sucked the life blood out of each other. They will never move. They can't even agree on a reliable form of contraception, let alone a new house. At least Phil and Kirsty are being paid to deal with them. Turn the fuck'n shit off — and live.

Can you believe you will actually sit there through interminable commercial breaks saying to yourself, 'Will they buy it this time? They do seem to like it.' 'Oh, that's perfect for them!'

And then, all of a sudden after 10 or so of these programmes, Graham and Phenella actually purchase a house. You are elated. You have just watched people buy a house. That's all. That's it. Nothing more.

But wait . . . As the credits roll, two months later, as they were about to finalise, Phenella had second thoughts. The clothes line was too close to the piggery after all. They like what they have seen, though, and are planning another trip to Spain to look again at the converted barn. Fuck me.

These programmes constantly recap what you have seen to grab new viewers and promote an exciting development that may be yet to come. May. No guarantees.

Like *Seven Sharp*. You will be watching mindless shit as they hook you with a long-winded promise of something possibly fantastic that may change the way you live forever. The fact is, these programmes are just stopping you from living now!

Coming up . . . Has Mavis from Panmure discovered a cure for diabetes in her back garden? Let's face it, if she has, the first you hear of it will not be on *Seven Sharp*! At least with programmes like *Seven Sharp* it's probably fresh dross every night.

Why not just take the shit car for a drive, eat a bad burger and swill it down with a cheap wine? Now that's real reward.

40

ANECDOTE:

I was recently transfixed by an English programme called something like *Storage Hoarders*. It featured two separate couples who each had a storage unit filled with items. These people were perfectly ordinary people. They were not obsessive; they just had a storage unit. The host, also very ordinary, and, dressed in an ill-fitting gown best-suited to storage, described how desperate their situation was. Not desperate at all, so far as I could tell. Anyway, the show opened up their units with the intention of ridding them of their past and transforming their lives by adding cash to their bank accounts.

For your benefit I will now turn this marathon into a sprint.

Couple one: father and son. Sold one set of drums for £550. Rosewood table, failed to get a bid perhaps due to a missing leg. Stamp collections valuation proved that collecting stamps had been a disastrous endeavour; no sale. Storage unit, almost intact.

Couple two: husband and wife. Sold nothing. None of their shit attracted a bid at all. Did throw some crap out. Storage unit, almost intact.

The host, looking like a wall-flower at a community dance in the 1970s, exclaimed how their lives had been turned around and that they were that much closer to their dream holidays.

Indeed, the only gem to come from this episode (and I am sure the whole series) of *Storage Hoarders* was a revelation to me. A standard storage unit can cost almost £3,000 a year. That was 40-minutes-going-on-a-lifetime well spent!

You can't watch this stuff. You just can't. It's worse than *The Hobbit*.

SUPPLEMENTARY ANECDOTE:

Many years after I left the hideous council flat I lived in with my mother on an estate in Bristol, I returned to remind myself of my life's journey. I met the couple who were living in the flat and had lived there for the past 21 years. It was small and truly awful. A tiny, tiny view of this amazing world. I went inside to find that they had installed a huge flat-screen TV. It was almost bigger than the wall it was hung on. They had been sitting there watching *Avatar*. The tree-clad world at war, populated with giant naked blue creatures, was the perfect escape from their lives. Perfect.

I wonder if they had a storage unit.

CLEANLINESS IN FAST-FOOD OUTLETS

Let's get one thing straight: this is still New Zealand. Just because you can buy a poppadum or shish kebab on the corner of every street, it shouldn't mean you can get botulism as easily.

I remember when a trip to a restaurant or takeaway in our country could mean one of only three things: steak and chips, fish and chips, or egg and bacon. Very nice, but it was time for some experimentation that didn't come from the *Edmonds Cookery Book*. So the introduction of different cultures and their food is fantastic, but it should be done to our standards. Our standards. The old ones of cleanliness, I am talking about here. You can get brilliant Indian food cooked in beautiful kitchens in the smart parts of Mumbai, so why do we have outlets that look like they are straight out of the Dakar slums?

The councils have much to answer for here. Listen up. If your health certificate is not an A it could be a B, meaning you were an A but something slipped up and you are on a warning to shape up or be closed down. The B should have to be prominently displayed and worn on your establishment as a badge of shame. There! Easy. I have invented a perfect system. Essentially, if you can't run an A establishment, you can't run a food establishment at all in this country. So fuck off!

'Oh, but what about our mother and our brother's wife and children? How will they survive if we have to close down? Not to mention our own children . . .' owners might say through an interpreter. Tough! You can't sell prescription medicine in New

Zealand without being either a chemist or a member of Black Power, so why should you be able to peddle food in filth?

Who in their right minds would go into any establishment with anything less than a B? Why do we have Cs, Ds and beyond? Close them down. The council officers know who these filthy people are, and seem to try endlessly to coax them towards hygiene. If they don't understand the need for it, don't coax them — close them! It's our health we are talking about. Maybe the health inspectors are getting an extra fillet or scoop? They should lose their jobs if they are not doing them properly. Shit, this is getting me worked up. How is it possible that some of these shit-holes are passed as anything above a Z?

It is not just the small foreign-food establishments, either. As you must know, filthy standards are creeping in and taking hold in many areas of the food industry. Our standards are slipping in general. Yours are, too. It's conditioning. You might still be relatively clean, but your tolerance for filth is growing as society gets dirtier.

So, let's mention some of the big names in catering.

And here's a tip: if you would love to backpack
through Third World countries but are unable to, due to budget constraints, worry no more. The Third World experience is right here on your doorstep.

Pop a bag of wet-wipes in your rucksack and call into McDonald's out by Auckland Airport. Not in the airport, but that newish area around it. I don't go there anymore, and maybe you will be disappointed, perhaps they have cleaned it up. The last time I was there, I was disgusted. Yes, they were busy, but that's their game. There was food and crap all over the floor and, worse, on the tables and seats. As I stood in awe of the filth, a female (I think!) staff member in a dirty smock walked with blinkers past umpteen filthy tables to one table, and, brandishing a dirty, wet cloth, rearranged the crumbs with a trusting moist swing of her fat arm, pushed a chair more or less straight, and marched back behind the food preparation area. What a shit-hole. No excuse, McDonald's. I witnessed it and, even if that was a one-off, you should be ashamed.

Let's even things up and bring in Mr Sanders' outfit! KFC in Cambridge. OMG, KFC. WTF?! I went in on a Sunday night on the way down to Napier. The floor was covered in wrappers, dirty tissues and containers, plus — naturally enough — food. Some uneaten, but partially chewed. The tables and chairs were covered in food bits, and you could see in the corners of booths where rubbish had been kicked in an attempt to cover up complete inadequacy. Standing, centre-stage in the seating area, was a dirty dustpan and brush. Why, I don't know. Perhaps KFC are trialing a self-clean idea in Cambridge. If so, not so good! The toilets were worse, but only because the waste was more offensive. Totally unacceptable, and, like the other example, even if this was a one-off, you should be ashamed.

ANECDOTE:

My father came home excited one evening from work when I was about nine years old. He said to my mother, 'Get dressed — we're going out.' He told me that we were going to get something to eat from an amazing and wondrous place, the likes of which I had never seen. It had just opened that day, and the food was so special that the recipe was kept secret from even the people who worked there. I was so excited, and my excitement grew as we came close to what was I think the first Kentucky Fried Chicken in New Zealand. Surrounded by New Zealanders in awe, we eventually got inside this food palace and I tasted the best food I had ever eaten. Enduring memories!

ANECDOTE 1A:

My father announced one evening that we were going out for dinner, and, even though I had my pyjamas on, we could still go because we did not have to leave the car. And, he said, we were not taking the food with us. It was blowing my young mind: if we were not taking food, but were eating food and were not getting out of the car . . . How would that ever work? How do we get the food into the car? What the jizicers was going on!

I could see the big Georgie Pie sign, but we drove in a different way. Next thing, my father asked me what I wanted, and we were actually talking from the car to a person who then passed the food, the actual food, through the open window into our car. Drinks and all! I say again: jizicers!

Turns out it was New Zealand's first drive-through. My dad loved firsts!

ANECDOTE 2:

I was once in Kabul. Taliban rule was a very fresh memory, and new freedoms were being explored with unease but enthusiasm everywhere, under the watchful, and at times inept, eyes of the United Nations, foreign military and do-gooders from everywhere.

Someone — maybe taking the piss, or perhaps just a clever opportunist — opened at some expense . . . Afghan Fried Chicken. AFC. Their by-line was 'Clean and Tasty!' It was in every way a take-off of KFC: the building, place mats, menus, food and design. I went in and was confronted by the AFC definition of 'clean'. The place had been open only about a month, but was already covered in dirt that would take years to be so ingrained in our country. The uniforms had never been cleaned, and right on the

48

counter was a wet mop. On the counter where you order, in front of the gentleman asking me what I wanted from their illuminated menu, a dirty, wet mop was oozing dark grey liquid that trickled down the counter. I ate heartily. I had allowed my strict hygiene standards to slip.

Two surprises were in store. One, it tasted fantastic. Two, it stayed down. I know: no problems, even though everything about the meal shouted *Campylobacter*.

POSSIBLE FACT:

I was told AFC was destroyed by a bomb a month or so after I ate there. Not surprising. A step too far too fast, perhaps.

ADJACENT FACT:

Public toilets are more of a disgrace now than they have ever been in New Zealand. What the fuck do these animals live like in the burrows they call home?

COOKBOOKS

Walk into almost any bookshop, any book section of any department store. Basically go anywhere books are stored, and there will be shelf upon shelf of new cookbooks. They are the most beautiful and expensive of books on the market. As the book industry reduces costs to try and stay viable in these changing times, cookbooks are becoming more lavish and costly to produce and buy. But why does anyone need another cookbook? (Stupid question. No one needs another cookbook.) No one to the best of my knowledge is inventing new ingredients, just subtle new ways of juggling them around. And that's if you are lucky . . . Mostly it is just the same thing on different china!

If you have cookbooks at your place, you must already have more than you need. What are you doing with them? Do you sit around all day looking at glossy pictures of food? If so, why? What the hell is wrong with you? You can starve to death looking at food!

Some of my favourite acquaintances are wonderful chefs. Sean Connolly, Peter Gordon, Al Brown, Annabelle White. They have all published umpteen cookbooks, and I am sure are currently working on yet more. Stop now, guys! Enough already. Back to the kitchen!

As for Jamie Oliver, Nigella what's-her-name, and any winner or runner-up from *MasterChef*, either they have produced too many books already, or have nothing to add, or both. If from this moment in time no new cookbooks were released, the world would not be the poorer.

Bonus! If you can't beat them, join them! I present to you yet another picture of food you will never be able to recreate in your kitchen, thus making this book as useful a cookbook as any other you have purchased lately.

Here's a tip: save your cookbook money and spend it in wonderful restaurants, actually eating amazing food. Then, if you must, take a damn picture of it when it arrives on the plate to look at later.

EXCEPTION:

If you are just a wanker and purchase cookbooks (or, for that matter, any books) just to pretty up the place and exude the aura of literacy about your glorious estate, good for you. Perception is often more important than reality.

ANECDOTE:

I said to my publisher, 'Look, is that another fuck'n cookbook? How many of these have you sold?'
    'Don't ask,' she replied.
  'Exactly,' I said. 'Too many fuck'n cookbooks!'
  To be fair, I was quietly hoping she would give me a copy . . .

LIST OF COOK BOOKS I HAVE:

NAME:	LOOKED AT THEM	USED THEM
	Y N	Y N
	Y N	Y N
	Y N	Y N
	Y N	Y N
	Y N	Y N
	Y N	Y N
	Y N	Y N
	Y N	Y N
	CIRCLE	

COSMETIC SURGERY

Apart from occasionally finding the results of cosmetic surgery outrageously entertaining, nothing much outrages me about it. So long as I am not going to be out of pocket as a result of your choices, go for it! It can look good, although the tendency some people have to become addicted and overdo it can negate the initial beauty benefits. If you want to disfigure yourself to the point Cirque du Soleil come calling, fantastic. Again, it's all part of the rich tapestry of life.

What I don't want to do, and let me stress this, is pick up the tab as a taxpayer for the stupid choices of others. If it turns to shit, pick up the tab yourself.

ANECDOTE:

Some years ago I would have coffee once or twice a week in a particular coffee shop. One day I walked in to find that one of the regular servers had turned into the Joker from *Batman*. She had always looked quite nice, I thought, and now she was a true freak. She seemed happy enough. She seemed not to notice the stares she was getting from genuinely astounded patrons. I hope she was okay with it. I loved it. It would be appalling if we all lived the same lives in the same bodies. She had given us all a gift of entertainment. She was less ordinary. More scary. I went in slightly more often for a while. So she sold more coffee.

55

FLYING

I remember the days of romance. The world was a much, much bigger place. And all its nooks and crannies were so very different, and were largely unspoiled from infiltration by each other. Travel was always exciting, and seemed to all those who didn't do it to be always risky. The old guard of global transport was moving aside. The mighty and majestic ocean liners were at the end of their heyday. The new vanguards of long-distance human reticulation had wings. The world belonged to Boeing. And everyone wanted a ride.

I know. Very fuck'n dramatic! But that was air travel. Shit, just a trip to the airport to wave someone off was an occasion to dress up for.

Things have sadly changed, and, just like the decline in good manners and the rise in the use of fuck-words, **air travel has become the preserve of the underclass.** As was entirely predictable, the underclass has rendered the experience of air travel to that of a bus trip through Pretoria. Even at my most economically depraved, I loved the remnants of the class system that survived the great revolution. It was to me aspirational. However, to most around me in the council flats and slums of industrial Bristol, success and wealth were seen as hopelessly unachievable and so something to resent. Sorry . . . where the fuck am I going with this?

Anyway, here's the thing: don't fly on shit, low-budget airlines. I have spent decades flying the globe and have become an expert on the best ways to passenger through the sky. As an international correspondent I travelled almost exclusively at the back of the plane. In more recent times, almost exclusively at the front. But regardless of economy or posh, the better the airline, the better, or more tolerable, the experience. Some of the very small airlines can produce exciting surprises, but the small airlines usually fly where choice is low or non-existent, so you will find what you find. It is the large airlines that differ so much in quality, and it is the large airlines that have plenty of competition. So why would you risk making an expensive, diabolically poor choice?

Here is my tip for a reliably well-above-average flight. Three words. Air. New. Zealand. There, the secret is out. It's ours, and it's pretty much the best. Air New Zealand have the best people and almost the best planes. They are amongst the cleanest and best maintained, and so are their aircraft. Yes, they can be more expensive, but usually not much more, and almost always much, much better and more reliable by a country mile. And they are ours. They are New Zealand in foreign lands, and it makes me proud to see them on far away runways. On one arrival at LAX in 2012, as my plane was pulling into its gate and I was all set to unclip the belt and project myself out of my seat so that I could be the person who has to stand waiting the longest, I saw the Air New Zealand plane with *The Hobbit* livery. God knows how many aircraft arrive there every day — maybe 5 million — but the ground staff were taking pictures of *The Hobbit* plane and pictures of each other in front of it. That's our airline. Excellence with attitude! (It was also the best part of the film.)

Supporting our airline is like supporting ourselves.

And supporting our promotion and future. But most of all it is about having the best flight you can get.

The very worst thing about Air New Zealand is also the best thing about United: they are in the same alliance. Air New Zealand should choose its bedfellows more wisely. Be very careful that lying with dogs doesn't see you rise with fleas!

ONLY POSSIBLE REASONS NOT TO FLY WITH AIR NEW ZEALAND:

1. You own another airline.
2. You have won tickets on another airline.
3. Air New Zealand don't fly to your destination.
4. You have vowed never to fly.
5. You are dysfunctional and obnoxious and may possibly want to travel at the same time to the same destination as me in business class.
6. You love being treated like an animal.
7. You are mad and desperate to experience PS on United. (For the meaning of 'PS', see later.)
8. You have a terminal aversion to clean planes.
9. You are desperate to arrive late, at the wrong destination.

QUESTIONS ABOUT AIR TRAVEL:

Why are people on planes so fuck'n stupid? 'We have three selections: jet planes (lollies), a cookie or chips.' How fuck'n hard is it to remember that? On a plane, very. If one more person next to me on a domestic flight asks, 'What do you have again?' you are going to need the flight marshal.

Why are people in so much of a hurry to open the overhead lockers when the plane stops? I want to be first!

Why do fuckers put their personal reading lights on and then go to sleep? You shits. Shits!

Why do you bring your children? Surely the constant crying is an indication that they don't like it, you other-passenger abusers!

Why on internal flights in the States do the fatties sit next to me and the really fat sit on me?

Why do I have to queue at all with other people? Don't you know who I am?

Why don't you know who I am?

Why do some people seem not to be able to smell themselves?

Whose fault is it that I am so intolerant?

PERSONAL — MY CAREER AS A PROFESSIONAL PILOT:

I had two flying lessons in a fixed-wing aircraft many years ago when I was still quite poor. I realised that I could not afford enough lessons, and thought that the cheapest way to get my flying licence would be to qualify in a glider and then upskill to powered flight. I had one lesson in a glider and almost vomited over the instructor. I can safely say it was the worst flying experience of my life. And that from someone who has flown EgyptAir many times, been in a plane crash, and travelled Jetstar! So, no more lessons, and the flying career of perhaps the best pilot ever was nipped in the bud! Instead I built a helipad in my garden and hoped for an influx.

ANECDOTE:

When you fly LA to New York, try JetBlue. Quite a good price and quite a pleasant airline. Get a late-night flight and there can be a bit of a party mood. Let's just say, as many purple potato chips washed down with as much Coke as you like. Do not fly American Airlines and do do do *not* fly United. I know you might get air points on your fuck'n Star Alliance card, but, believe me, it's not worth it. I was flighting much as a pig is carried to market with United and was experiencing PS first hand. PS? I hear you ask. What alluring product of the sky is that? Well, I called over an aged denizen of air travel. An old, fat, poorly groomed flight attendant by the name of Judy. Let's call her 'Dirty Judy'. (And not in a good way.) She reluctantly and slowly approached my unclean seat, and I leant over the enormous belly of a smelly fat man to ask the meaning of 'PS'. The letters adorned all of the soiled brochures in the ripped seat pocket lying on the floor by my feet. She scowled at me for a moment — or did she just pause, through a scowled face? 'It's "premium service",' she barked, and turned to leave. I interrupted the building momentum of her hooves with another brave and probing question. 'And am I experiencing that now?' I asked. She paused, much as a bull does the moment before he charges and plunges his mighty horns into your groin. Then Dirty Judy indignantly walked away, never to glance at me again.

Fuck'n shit airline. PS, my arse!

SUPPLEMENTARY ANECDOTE:

I arrived slightly late and during something of a war for a flight from an outback airstrip to Phnom Penh in Cambodia. Late, yes, but also that day's only passenger, so perhaps a little respect would have been nice. The terminal was still smoking from mortar attack, and there were a number of dangerous uncordoned-off holes in the floor. I afforded them a little grace. They were, after all, experiencing slight unrest. As the plane nervously waited on the runway, two poorly dressed but well-armed youth rifled through my belongings and checked my ticket. (Where is Mike McRoberts with a spare flak jacket when you need him?) I was about to walk to the plane when they informed me of the airport charge of US$25. I said, 'You have got to be fuck'n joking?' And with that they threw my bags in a discus-like motion towards the plane and the contents scattered everywhere. 'Move!' they shouted at me with guns pointed. 'You don't want to miss your plane, bastard.'

'Absolutely not,' I thought, but kept quiet.

Lesson: just pay the $25.

61

NOT ANOTHER FUCK'N ANECDOTE:

I was flying over the parched desert of Southern Sudan. The six-seater was full. Alarmingly, I was sitting in what would be the co-pilot's seat in a bigger aircraft. I could smell the Jim Beam wafting from every pore of the pilot, a rough old man in short-sleeved shirt and shorts. I think we were the only people on board who spoke English. During the flight I had been studying the instruments. 'I may need to land this,' I thought. 'This guy's not going to make it.' He was certainly behaving oddly. About what I judged to be half an hour or so from our destination, he turned to me and spoke the words no passenger wants to hear: 'Can you fly a plane?'

Normally my response to that question would be a somewhat arrogant 'God, I haven't flown for ages!', but on this occasion I chose a little more honesty. 'I can't fly a plane,' I said. 'Fuck,' he said.

Ten minutes passed and I plucked up the courage to enquire as to the meaning behind his question. He told me he had almost completely lost the feeling in his legs and would quite possibly require medical assistance prior to landing. I had already ascertained with a fair amount of certainty that no one else on the plane was going to be of any assistance, as, I am sure, had he. I told him I could fly the plane now, and he could do the best he could to massage the life back into his limbs for landing. He thought this was a great idea and handed me the controls with no words of wisdom. **I was a pilot at last.**

In the available space, he contorted his tired and alcohol-fuelled body. After some awkward twisting and rubbing, he reached the point where he thought he could land. We were in sight of the strip as he wedged himself in and I handed over the controls to my number two. We landed without incident, and I stood with some pride as my ramshackle cargo disembarked safely.

GENERALISATIONS

It is a fundamental cornerstone of communication: the ability to generalise rather than occupy huge amounts of time specifically itemising things and backing them up with concrete evidence. It is very economical and perfectly valid.

Example: Asians are bad drivers. Yes, they are. But, to many, true though that general statement is, it is offensive. Because they know an Asian — let's call him Xinhow — who is a good driver. It is not possible to name Xinhow and all the other good Asian drivers, who you don't know, in order to reassert that, as a proportion of bad drivers, Asians are more than holding their own. You see? Nothing wrong with generalisations at all.

So the next time you rudely interrupt someone in a pious tone, thinking you are correcting them, with a line like, 'There are actually some quite nice homes there!', just know this: you are a nit-picker. And your revelation has done nothing but slow down a conversation or monologue that quite correctly included the generalisation **'Otara is a shit-hole'.**

It is not necessary to flag that you are generalising. If the person or people you are talking with are too stupid or corrupted by their own prejudices to understand, you should save your breath.

SUPPLEMENTARY EXAMPLE:

Fat people just eat too much!
Really? My clinically obese Uncle Hohepa has a disease that prevents him from metabolising food the way we do. He is trapped in a body he can't control . . .
Give me strength!

HOMOSEXUALS

Why is it that so many homosexuals allow themselves to be defined by their sexuality? It's just bizarre. So often they campaign to be treated like everyone else, when their whole persona is captivated by homosexual affectations. I have found this to be more true of males than females. So many gay men act like they have just finished a shift on the men's apparel floor at Grace Brothers. I know it must have been hard at school, but get over it! Move on.

I have been accused of being homophobic in the past, but I have also been accused of being homosexual. Again proving that I am a perfectly balanced human being. (On one occasion I was stopped in the street in Australia by a fan. The bloke said how much he liked me on air. I introduced him to my girlfriend, who was standing next to me, and in true Aussie style he flinched and said, 'Shit, mate, I always thought you were a homo! Good on ya!')

Homosexuals have to understand this: you are not special just because you are gay. The world does not need to stand aside and recognise you for your ability to have sex with your own kind. It's not a skill. A party trick, perhaps, but not a skill. You don't need to show off your sexuality in public, it's not clever. And you certainly don't need special treatment from others. Making homosexuality a circus act is entirely counter-productive.

Now it's time for me to use the line 'Some of my best friends are . . .' Well, they are. And for the most part you wouldn't instantly know they are, because they are getting on with their lives as human beings not sexual freaks. Having said that, I do have some close friends who are sexual freaks.

I have long been of the opinion that we all fit somewhere

between 100 per cent heterosexual and 100 per cent homosexual. To explain my hypothesis I have created a diagram:

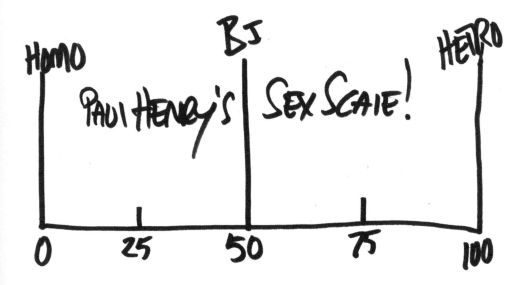

On this scale of 0–100, 0 is completely homosexual and 100 completely heterosexual. Therefore 50 is completely bisexual. In my vast life experience, it seems to me few if any are either 0 or 100. Arguably, the higher your score the more 'normal' you are. I concede that the closer you are to 50 the more fun life could be!

So where are you?

If this is your book, pop your name on the line and your score in the box.

As this is also my book I will fill my score in too.

You see: dangerously close to having a great deal of fun indeed.

Those who have called me homophobic in the past will be eating their words now. Those who have accused me of being homosexual will feel at least partly vindicated.

YOUR NAME: _____

YOUR SCORE: ☐

MY NAME: PAUL HENRY _____

MY SCORE: 67

ANECDOTE:

When I was in my late teens, early twenties, I worked at the BBC, mostly in Bristol, England. As you can see from my BBC ID, I could have been viewed as something of a drawcard to predators with sexual intent. Indeed they did exist in some not insubstantial number, but my personality was such that I batted them off with gay abandon.

I was actually taken out to a gay establishment by Quentin Crisp. That is my very biggest run-in with homosexual royalty. But perhaps the loveliest gay-related story I have from that time took place in a jeweller's shop on Park Street in Bristol.

I was walking home from work and called in to look at watches I could never have afforded. It was a big flash jeweller's and quite intimidating. There were two old ladies prowling through a tray of rings under the watchful and stern supervision of a dark-suited sales gentleman. After some time the bell on the front door rang as a magnificently dressed man swept in with a small and sycophantic entourage. The man was actually wearing a black cape with a black velvet hat, a silk scarf, and carrying a cane. I was standing quite close to the old women and could easily hear them saying, 'Look, look, it's him. That one from that show!' They were both very excited.

At the same time the sales assistant rudely folded away their ring tray and abandoned them. He called for extra help and walked over to the entourage. 'Good afternoon, Mr Inman. Thank you so much for coming in, sir. How can we be of service?'

The old women had missed the rudeness and were overcome with excitement. John Inman was at the height of his fame, and I, too, was somewhat star-struck (67!). However, clearly Inman had not missed the rudeness, or for that matter the excitement of his female crowd. He did not answer the salesman, but paused and walked directly over to the women. He smiled at me (67!!), turned to the old ladies and said, 'It should not be hard to find rings for such beautiful women', and as they melted in his presence he beckoned over a different salesman. I left the shop some time later with Inman still helping his fan base find a ring. They were having the time of their lives. He was a true gentleman.

RELATED COMMENT:

Theatrical gays can be quite fun.

69

IMMIGRATION

Do you ever wonder how some people managed to migrate to New Zealand? I do!

I am reasonably happy with our refugee policy. Reasonably. I do have deep concerns, though, with the desire of some in our country to obey without question the directives of the **United Nations.** It can utter the most **ridiculous** statements at times. And, quite frankly, any organisation that elevates a country like Sudan to a position of global influence must be phenomenally flawed. So far as giving a voice to the dangerous fool of a leader of Iran, I can see why it does, but God give me strength! Suffice to say, the United Nations is no better than a necessary evil.

There is a simple test we must apply to everyone seeking to immigrate to our beautiful country. Are they people we need, or people who need us? If the latter, the answer to their application must be no.

It seems to me that we hunt globally for nutters, the needy, and those who are likely to cluster. How ridiculous! Part of the test should be their desire and ability to integrate into our society. If they can't speak English, how can they integrate? If they are not prepared to learn English prior to their application, they clearly have no desire to integrate. Answer: no!

New Zealand is a very desirable country in which to live. And we should welcome those who will contribute positively. The more positively, the easier it should be for them to gain access. So far as bringing family, the same test should apply. If you choose

NZ IMMIGRATION TEST.

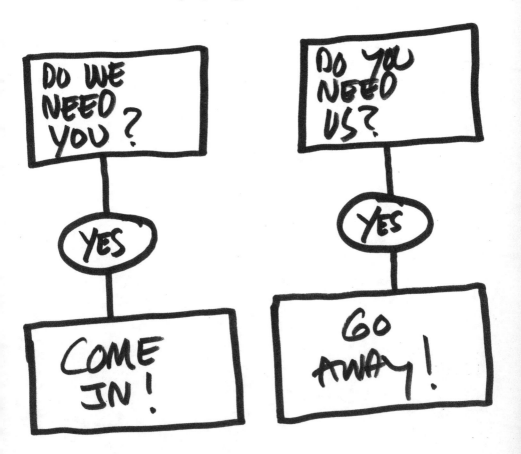

to migrate to another country and your family can't get in: your choice, not the country's. Tough!

NOTE TO MIGRANTS:

This is New Zealand, not the country you are seeking to abandon. You have chosen this country for the life benefits it affords. Be part of enforcing these and improving our lifestyle for us all. Do not try and recreate a compound of the life and country you have left behind. If you have no interest in being an active, positive part of our beautiful land, bugger off. If do you have an interest, thank God for you.

72

IPADS

I understand the point of the iPad. Invent a new device that fits a new section of an existing market that you have created for the sole purpose of exploiting. It is the sort of concept Hitler would have come up with had he not been forced into that bunker with that awful Braun woman. (So awful was she that he was forced to kill himself after less than 40 hours of marriage.) Anyway, Hitler, Jobs. You get the point.

The key thing in being successful with this strategy is that you must not create a device that is so capable that it replaces one you are already exploiting. And so we have the most frustratingly useful bit of electronic crap on the planet. The iPad is to writing what handcuffs are to sculpture. Why is it so bloody shitty?!

I concede I have made no attempt to upskill myself on the subtle nuances of the iPad's operating thing, but for Christ's sake, it's 2013. The thing should just be perfect. Shit!

ANECDOTE:

I have just realised: it's NOT 2.30pm yesterday. My iPad is on LA time. Bloody bastard thing — trying to sabotage my whole day.

So I went into settings and typed 'Auckland' — just Auckland — and instantly it updated the time and date. Quite clever!

QUESTION:

Why are apostrophes on a different screen? Shit!

7

74

LOUIS VUITTON

It's a fine balance in a luxury shop between sophisticated and classy, and just poncey and snobby. The big chains like LV, Prada and Tiffany's mostly get it spot-on. They know you can't always judge a book by its cover. Sometimes the most unlikely looking and even behaving visitors to their stores can be big purchasers. But they are selling an experience as well as a product, so it needs to be a notch or two up on Kmart. And at their prices it needs to be rolled in glitter.

I am just as at home in either environment. But I think that, perhaps as a direct result of being at the very bottom of the social ladder for quite some time when I was young, I do like a nice environment and good service. However, for the same reason, I do expect quality. If I am paying a shit-load of money for something, I expect it to be perfect.

So, I went into Louis Vuitton to get a briefcase. I knew exactly the style I was after. I went into two LV stores and found the perfect one. Not the all-leather one for US$9,850 plus tax, but the half-canvas half-leather one for US$5,400 plus tax. Lucy, my eldest daughter, was with me and could see that I was about to buy it. It was so much nicer than the all-leather one, and with tax would still have been under US$6,000. You know, it was a thing of true beauty, and a pleasure, almost an honour, to hold. The male attendant could also see I was about to buy it, as he had one (and only one) so untouched that it still had the protective plastic on the silver catches. Then he said that the complimentary key case would be engraved for free with my initials, and we all knew that I was about to part with a lot of money. Even the two suited security guards. I almost frothed at the mouth at the thought of getting anything for free at Louis Vuitton. That, like, never happens. I looked in the mirror, under the salesman's instruction, to see just how good I looked holding it, despite the appalling clothes I was wearing above my jandals.

It was at that moment I noticed that one of the catches holding the handle was not fitted in line with the others or the pattern. I couldn't see anything else now but this fuck-up. How did this bag get past the craftsman's expert eye? Was he even a craftsman, or had this one been slapped together during lunch by the janitor?

I couldn't see beyond it. I said to Lucy, 'Look, is that in line?' At once the salesman said that the bags were all made by hand and everything about the bag was   in perfect line.   He pointed out the rivets and how they were in perfect line. They were. All of them.   In perfect line.

Lucy went quiet, and then said, 'It's crooked.'

The salesman said, 'That's not possible.' He held it upright, and almost without inspection said, 'It's perfect!'

I said to Lucy, 'Is it just me?'

She said, 'No. It's not in line.'

The man rotated the case and inspected it fully. He went very quiet.

We left the store with an unbelievable feeling. How can that happen at Louis V?

Fuck'n outrage!

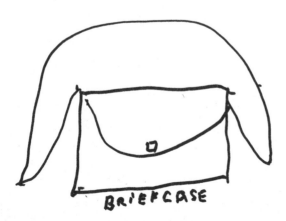

BRIEFCASE

CONUNDRUM:

So what do you do? There are so few of these cases that you will have to order one in. But the experience has been tarnished. A hell of a lot of the glitter has fallen off. Even if they offered a substantial discount, you can't buy it. 'Here's my near-perfect LV case. It was only $4,000, because the handle is crooked.' You'd have to be mad!

You can't buy that one. You'd always be looking at the fault. Is it getting worse . . . ? Then there's the hideous chance that someone else who has just said to you, 'OMG, is that what I think it is?' then says, 'Shit, the handle is crooked.'

You have to walk away and, as I did, purchase an attaché case from an exclusive English company at half the price.

As for that LV store in Las Vegas, I hope they sent the case to LV HQ with a stern letter. But I do wonder if they put it back on the shelf.

QUESTION:

Is there an Asian gentleman wandering the strip in Vegas with poker chips and cash stuffed in a Louis Vuitton attaché with a crooked handle?

SUGGESTION TO LV:

Sort out your quality control. You should be fuck'n ashamed of yourselves.

MAORI ACTIVISTS

The old saying 'united we stand, divided we fall' is pretty well accurate, as are many old sayings. I am hard-pressed to think of a country with a separatist motivation that is spectacularly successful.

New Zealand is a small and vulnerable nation. It suffers from the tyranny of distance and isolation from markets, as well as from a perilously small economy. And as economic conditions around the globe change, our country must adapt to succeed, or die. Despite considerable challenges and at times questionable governance, we are extraordinarily well regarded globally. New Zealand is a success, with a very high standard of living, and any reasonable person with an understanding of the world would regard it as a great place to live.

Sadly, there are many in New Zealand who are not reasonable and who have little understanding of the world. Maori activists/separatists are among them. Essentially, these ungrateful fools are sabotaging our nation. New Zealand has an excellent record on human rights. It is an inclusive country with extraordinarily good services provided more than fairly, and it has a history of colonisation we should be proud of. Should. But are we? No. Instead, many wowsers fall over themselves to apologise for the past. To call for compensation. And many are demanding compensation and special status. Damn the consequences. Damn the future.

Did everything in the past run smoothly? No. Were some people exploited and abused? Yes. Should this be acknowledged and in some cases compensated for? Yes, probably. But let's recognise what we are doing here: we are building a country. We are in this together for our futures and those of our children, and we need to be pulling together and pulling our weight. All of us should be pulling our weight.

Most Maori activists I have met are in it for themselves. Many have created a nice little earner in lieu of actually working. If they are so hell-bent on living in the past, surely they should be crediting the European colonisers for their fundamentally good stewardship? Saving the natives from themselves and from more hostile nations. They should celebrate our country for the opportunities it supports and the lifestyles it fosters. But no. These disgruntled troublemakers don't want to be part of our future, or for that matter part of any solution. They want everything and bugger the cost and consequences. They are destroyers, not creators.

They should be called to account. What good do they do? Who are they working for and for what ultimate purpose? Governments make payouts that can't be afforded on behalf of the taxpayer. Both Maori and non-Maori. And where does the money go? Who actually benefits and who is held accountable? The more separate we become, the more divided we are, the greater the chance we fall. And if we do, the irony is that we will all fall together.

The next time someone tries to tell you that New Zealand should have a separate legal system or health system or any separate system, or that they should be compensated for something that was done to someone who is long dead by someone who is long dead, tell them you are too busy building a country to listen to their ignorant negative bullshit.

NOTE TO MAORI ACTIVISTS:

Get a real job. Take advantage of the extraordinary opportunities that exist, and build your and our capacity. Appreciate how good things are. Improve the environment for yourself, our community and your children, and teach them to dream big and be positive about their futures with limitless goals.

Look into the eyes of your children and ask yourself if this is the best you can do for them — fostering a foundation of disgruntlement and reciting excuses for failure.

NOTE TO GOVERNMENT:

Harden the fuck up. Now!

MARINELAND NAPIER

Marineland in Napier was **iconic.** Perhaps still is, even though it was closed due to the lack of a dolphin or six in 2008. Officially, it is 'closed to the public', but who or what it *is* open for is a mystery to me. If a public attraction is closed to the public, let's just call it as it is — closed.

By the way, if there is one thing that outrages me more than the closure of Napier's Marineland it is the rampant over-use of the word 'iconic', especially in the media. However, in this case, and every case when the word is used by me, it is correct. (Note: 'The iconic Cloud on Auckland's waterfront' — I don't think so. Whatever media outlet it was that uttered that line should be hauled before the ridiculous broadcasting standards thing! The correct line should have been: 'The abomination of a temporary structure known as the Cloud on Auckland's waterfront . . .')

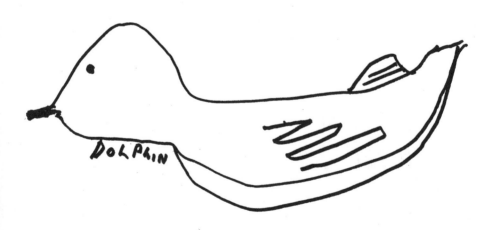

So, back to the precious dolphins and their environmentally obsessed supporters. What makes a dolphin's life more precious than that of a cow or a sheep or for that matter an ant? Buddha, a very wise sage of foreign extraction, would have us believe there is no difference at all. Having said that, ancient scripts show he may never have tried moving a flock of sheep into a race!

Yes, like fur seals, dolphins are very cute. Not quite as cute, but still up there on the scale of cute. They do seem friendly and helpful and smart. But get close and they smell! Fact.

The most important thing to note is: dolphins are not like us. They don't run the world. We do. They don't seem to have an insatiable appetite to be entertained through the exploitation of other living creatures like us. Well, that's just the way it is. Hunt some more down, squeeze them into a tank and make them dance. Now that's entertainment!

Okay, so let's be humane. It needs to be a nice tank and we need to treat them well. We don't need to hunt them down from the wild, we just need to buy them from a dolphin farm, like one of the SeaWorlds in the United States.

Stupid Napier councillors buckled under pressure. They could not see the huge benefit from investing in the historically significant tourist attraction in their town. They allowed Marineland to pivot on the life of one old dolphin, Kelly. And when Jesus pulled the plug on Kelly, the power went out on the park.

We were told that times had changed. People don't want to see things penned up now. We want to swim in the wild with these majestic carnivores and look at them from boats travelling at a safe distance. Safe, of course, for the dolphins. Well, that's all crap. Yes, we might like those things, but go to the fantastic aquarium in Atlanta or to SeaWorld in San Diego and you will find the happiest dolphins in the world. You will also find thousands upon thousands of excited people learning about the wonders of the deep and actually getting the environmental message.

People being entertained by dolphins, who are themselves being entertained by people.

So what Napier needed was more dolphins, not no dolphins. Actually what Napier needed was a majority on the council who had the foresight to say, 'We are going to have a Marineland which will be as important to our future as it was to the past. It won't be a drain on the ratepayer. It will be a financial and social windfall.'

What an outrageous waste of an opportunity. You dopey bastards.

ANECDOTE:

I f you never visited Napier Marineland, leave the following lines blank. If you are among the hundreds of thousands who have happy memories from the park, write a note about it here:

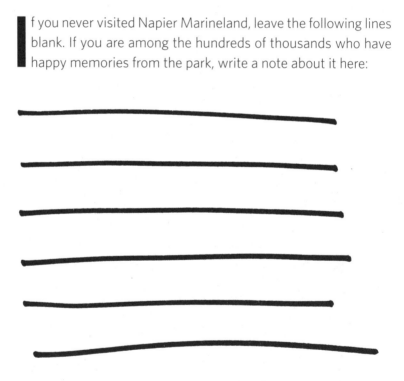

You see, that's what makes a thing iconic!

POSSIBLE FACT:

E very dolphin in the wild has heard of marine parks and wants in.

85

MUSLIMS

Here's the thing: the biggest difference between those staunch in the Muslim faith and pretty much everyone else, from a religious perspective, is that Muslims are playing a long game. The longest of all religious games currently on the table in the world. If winning in the religious stakes is your aim (and it is their aim), the Muslim religion is in the box seat and I know why.

It is because they show little tolerance to other religions but insist tolerance is shown to them. It is because they do not modify and adapt in the same way most other religions do. Thus, as other religions are forced to evolve their beliefs in order to, they would say, 'stay relevant', the Muslim religion stands firm. And in the end, sheer numbers will bring success. So you breed and infiltrate. Dispersing throughout the non-Muslim world in what, to all intents and purposes, could be entirely non-threatening to most.

In the non-Muslim world, people are mostly only interested in the short game, or self-gratification. It is easier to be compliant and welcoming than it is to challenge and confront. And, after all, non-Muslims are adapting their religions and societies anyway. That's why Muslims can do in our country what Christians could never do in a staunch Muslim country.

EXAMPLE:

They can be raped without having to go to jail for it.

FURTHER EXAMPLE:

They can go to the bank with their faces covered. You try banking in Saudi in your bikini!

You could argue that a religion that is prepared to adapt as much as the Christian religion has over the past few decades, in particular the past decade, must either have been wholly wrong in the first place or alternatively just opportunistic, more interested in its own survival than in its fundamental teachings. After all, when did Christ change his mind and say women could be trusted speaking to congregations? When did he say you should dob in child molesters within your own ranks, or that it is okay for people with the same body parts to join in wedlock? Christianity is like Lego, it can change into anything so long as you are prepared to wait a bit for new pieces to be released!

So, back to the Muslims. In the end, will we all be Muslim? And would that be a bad thing? I don't want to be, but that's because I love the short game and self-gratification too much.

If we were all Muslims, would the world be a better place or a complete shit-hole? So the big question is this: is it ultimately a good thing that we are so tolerant of the Muslim faith in New Zealand?

ANECDOTE:

Several years ago I found myself deep in the Ugandan countryside experiencing their mostly unique culture, albeit a primarily English-speaking, Christian culture. I was driving one day down a narrow, pot-holed, snake-riddled jungle road, when all at once I came upon a . . . Coca-Cola factory. It was fairly new. Huge, ugly and so out of place. Everywhere people were drinking the stuff and basking quite literally in the reflected glory of Coke signs. I said to Bamyon Naglay, my companion in the car, 'It's getting more and more like Atlanta here every day.' And as the sun set on the banks of the Limpopo River, we talked over a delicious sugary beverage about the way, in the end, the world would be the same wherever you went. We decided that was a bad thing, ate our hot dogs and went to sleep.

This has subsequently become known as the Henry Naglay Global Sameness Theory, or HNGST.

NUDITY

So, taking all your clothes off and walking around like it's normal in front of strangers who are also naked, is that weird or what? Actually, it's mostly not weird. So long as it is warm, I love it. Does that make me a nudist? Yes, I meet some of the criteria. I like to swim, sunbathe and just be naked when it makes sense to be. There are days at home when I find it hard to summon the desire to put on clothes. Reporters have come to my door and I have slung a towel around myself as my only protection from their inept storytelling.

Over recent years I have started to frequent nudist establishments in the United States. They call them 'clothing optional', but the freakiest people are the ones who keep their clothes on at those places. What are they up to? The reason I gravitate to these places in the USA is that the weather there is perfect for it. And let's be clear: I don't take my clothes off in public for some desire to be naked at all times during all activities. This may mean I am not a proper nudist. I don't want to be cold. That's one of the things clothes are best at: keeping you warm. I don't want to get scratched. Another good reason to wear clothes: protection. I just like to swim and generally relax naked in the sun with other people who don't care that you are naked because they are mature enough to understand that there is nothing to it. It is no big deal. What are people trying to hide? Only things we can all predict are there: vaginas, penises, breasts, etc. (Why did I say 'etc'? Oh yes, my favourite — **bottoms!**)

The fact is that very few people are looking at you anyway. And you are looking at very few people. I have found that most nudists

89

are almost completely consumed with their own looks, far too consumed to care what others look like. Or alternatively, like me, they just don't give a damn. They enjoy being naked and don't consider it in the slightest.

Once you take the clothes off, somehow the conversation seems to improve with total strangers. Odd, but it's like, 'This is just me, nothing to hide . . . Have a chat.' You do find yourself making lots of eye contact.

Swimming and just 'being' when you are naked is so relaxing and natural.

Of course there are people you can't help but notice, but you notice them in the same way you would if you were clothed. The very fat, the very beautiful. You just see them and think 'Wow', and get back to living.

The clothed are quick to judge nudists, in many cases as deviants. That's an outrage. Often this comes from the fact that they themselves are hung up on how they look. In general, people are very hung up on how they look to others, and mostly it's just not that important. And when it comes to nudity, most people are very hung up. Get over yourself and visit one of these places. Take all your clothes off and feel the confidence you get by abandoning your inhibitions in front of strangers who have abandoned theirs.

Choosing the best establishment is a bit like choosing the best cruise. With cruising, you have ships for the young party set at one extreme, through to cruises for the almost dead at the other. With nudist establishments, there are those for the sporty, the sexually hungry, the homosexual, the spiritual and so on. Get the choice wrong and things can be interesting, dull, outrageous or — in the case of the spiritual — bloody annoying.

So I get pissed off with people who judge others because of their own prejudices. Because they are different. In this case that covers the judgmental dressed. I also get pissed off with the precious. And, bizarrely, I have bumped into many precious nudists. The thing is, there is nothing clever about taking your clothes off in public. The whole point is that it is natural. And yet there are those, many of them classing themselves as spiritual or environmentally in touch, who seem to view nudism as close to God. They parade around in a trance-like, holier-than-thou state. Drifting around between workshops and therapies. They float each other around in the hot pools and just get in the fuck'n way. They hum and sort of chant . . . What the fuck?

Again, choose the right establishment. Some are so precious that they don't allow any technology, phones or laptops, etc. Worse, some don't allow alcohol. How ridiculous is that? I love the ones with the extended happy hours.

AROUSAL:

Most clothing optional establishments have tips for first-timers. Clearly, having read these tips, one of the biggest concerns men must have is what to do with an unwanted erection. The tips say something like, 'Just slip into the pool until it subsides.' To be frank I have never experienced an unwanted erection. All of mine have been welcomed with open arms!

MY TIP FOR THE FIRST-TIMER:

Remember: no one is looking at you.

EXECUTIVE SUMMARY ON NUDITY:

It's no big deal!

ANECDOTE:

One of those life experiences you will probably never forget is the first time you visit a nudist establishment. I was in Mammoth in California. I was on a road trip and had driven that day from Las Vegas, an amazing drive that takes you through Death Valley into the mountains. So you see desert, mountains and forest, in both extreme heat and snow. The next day was going to take me through the centre of Yosemite National Park, but a large section of road was closed due to snow. The best alternative route was to zigzag between California and Nevada towards Sacramento. A great road trip, but who wants to spend a night in Sacramento? Not me!

I had recently been told of a commune-like spa named Harbin Hot Springs in the bush north of San Francisco, so I called them and booked in for three nights. The communal aspect alarmed me, so I booked the most expensive and exclusive accommodation they had available. I am not a great sharer of things like accommodation! To be fair I had been told it was clothing optional by people who are not nudists, but they said the hot springs were fantastic and, if you can cope with the resident hippie clan and so long as you didn't go on the weekend when it filled up with 'homosexuals on the hunt', it would be quite an experience and a relaxing stay. None of those things bothered me, so with some level of excitement and expectation I embarked on another great drive through America. After leaving Mammoth at about 10am, I found myself on a road of rapidly decreasing width and quality in thick bush with the GPS telling me I should 'turn around when possible' as I was not on a road at all. It was about 7pm. By now it was dark and just a little foreboding. In the back of my mind I was running through the scene in the movie *Wrong Turn* where he still had the chance to turn back but chose not to. What a twat! Blood-bath ensued.

I had just started to look at the fuel gauge in the way you do when you are completely lost, when a light appeared in the centre of the road ahead. As I drew close I could see it was a kind of sentry box, occupied by some sort of aging, **feral mammal** with dreadlocks, swaddled in a hessian throw. He looked like Dustin Hoffman at the halfway transformation mark in *Tootsie*. The small Harbin Hot Springs sign seemed a little redundant.

One of the most ironic things about these places, which you would assume were all about personal freedom, is the strict and seemingly endless chronicle of rules and regulations. Honest to God, even though I had booked in and driven a million miles in a day to get to this isolated oasis, mini Hagrid in the sentry box took me through the daunting list of dos and don'ts (mostly don'ts) one by one.

No cameras, no cellphones, no internet and — by far the most concerning — no alcohol. I had a boot full of cheap wine (sorry, trunk full of cheap liquor) and quite an appetite for a drink, but Dustin was deadly serious. Clothing optional came at quite a price. After following the map to the car park, I parked and looked again at the map. The paths were poorly lit, and clusters of hippie-like folk had gathered. It was quite a walk carrying inappropriate luggage past dormitory blocks and cottages to my accommodation. One of my bags was my banker's attaché case. Jesus Christ, I must have looked out of place.

Before I even opened the door to my room I had promised myself I would be leaving at first light and bugger the cost. On opening the door, it was confirmed — this was just not me. Let's just say the feral theme continued.

There was just time to make the communal dinner in the dining hall. I was in luck. This was the night the bush people came down from their huts with their offerings to share. Save me. After what was a far too healthy meal, I went for a swim. I just took all my clothes off in my room and paraded to one of the pools. At some point over the next few hours I was won over. It was a melting pot of endlessly interesting people who had no clothes on. The waters were brilliant and the experience priceless. I left at the last possible moment three days later with a complete tan.

THWARTING:

So, I had intended to make my point by publishing the following pictures of me naked with the following captions. My publishers were unsure as were some others, but I didn't care about their concerns. It seemed to me, given my views on nudity, that my credibility could be called into question if censored pictures accompanied my views. Essentially, I didn't give a damn what people thought. However, there are a very few people whom I care a great deal about and whose concerns are important to me. My daughters were horrified. (Mostly about what their friends would think!) In a way, their horror at the thought of their father publishing shots of his penis in his book is the perfect confirmation of my views. The next generation are already well repressed in the nudity stakes.

To all the ladies, and the men called Quentin, who are now devastated by the revelation that they were so close to seeing my manhood but at the final hurdle fell: sorry!

So anyway . . .

This is a picture of a chubby 52-year-old man at a 'clothing optional' (nudist) resort, Living Waters Spa, in Desert Hot Springs, 20 minutes from Palm Springs in California. The reason you can't see anyone else in the picture is that, for perhaps obvious (although somewhat ironic) reasons, cameras are not permitted. As a result of that, the photographer is the resort owner, Jeff, and the naked man is me.

Now I know, you might say almost anyone can appear naked in a published picture as an arse shot. So there's another picture of the same naked 52-year-old from a different angle on the next page.

Nothing that unusual: an aged male human body. Back to your homes . . . Nothing much to see here!

My mum.

Mum circumnavigates the Sky Tower at 80 years old.

Standing at the bow of my boat.

BOATING

Serious recreational boating is perhaps the very worst investment in entertainment you can make. If you are infected with the curse of a love of boating, you lose all financial perspective. Friends and family will say things like, 'Why don't you just rent a boat when you want to go out on the water?' That statement betrays their total lack of understanding. Clearly no salt water in those veins!

For me the line that best sums up the passion that is boating is this one: 'They were the best of times, they were the worst of times.'

It is a passion that gives and takes, sometimes simultaneously. It can easily cost you as much as, or more than, buying and running a house, but with no chance of capital gain. Quite the opposite in fact. Your vessel is deteriorating as you read this sentence. The deterioration can't be stopped. You just have to throw shit-loads of money at slowing it down.

It is outrageous that an intelligent person such as I am, who is capable of wisely investing and spending, can shit as much money as I do on boats. But as I write this, I am smiling at the thought of my current small ship just waiting in the marina to let me know what else needs fixing on her.

When a door latch breaks at your house, it can be fixed for, say, $50. The same problem on a boat will cost $500 to repair — and when they have finished, they are only 'almost' sure that it's fixed, and have spotted two other things that are looking dodgy! I think it was Dennis Conner who described yachting as like standing over the toilet, flushing money away. May have been someone else, but it pretty well sums it up. A great friend of mine, Peter Williams

QC, a man who has flushed a not inconsiderable amount of cash down the toilet on boats, describes blue-water sailing as like being in prison, but with the added risk of drowning. Both men are true boaties. They know, as I do, that life is not complete unless you have the escape vessel moored nearby.

The prize for the true boatie is in the ownership. Yes, you may hardly ever take her out. And yes, she may treat you like shit 90 per cent of the time. But she's yours. She is your total protection from Mother Nature. And when you are out at sea, there is nothing other than the grace of your ship and your stewardship of her that keeps you from floundering. It is raw and basic and fuck'n fantastic. It is living, and you can put a price on it: shit-loads of money!

EXERCISE FOR THE BOATIE:

Divide the total cost of annual ownership, including depreciation of your vessel, by the number of days you take her out. The figure you come up with should be approximately one-tenth of the cost of leasing a vessel four times as luxurious as yours for a day. If it is less, you are living the dream. If it is more, I salute you!

FACT:

I actually *love* my boat. As I have loved all of the boats I have owned while I have owned them.

SUPPLEMENTARY FACT:

I own two boats. The one I hardly ever use, and the one I never use. Reluctantly, I decided to sell the one I never use. I procrastinated for quite some months, took a long look at her while selecting photos for the sales brochure — and decided she was far too beautiful not to be mine!

ANECDOTE:

I was alone on the deck, leaving the Bay of Islands early one morning on the largest small ship I have ever owned. Auto-pilot on, I was standing on the bow as the sun rose. Perfect weather and sea for the trip back to Auckland. The engine was thumping away beautifully, and 40 tons of perfectly maintained vessel was sitting beneath my feet. As I rounded the rim of the bay, I was joined by six large dolphins on the bow wave. Rising and falling on the smooth swell, this was pure paradise. This was one of those cameo experiences that you need to remember when a diesel engineer is saying, 'Fuck, this looks bad!'

NOTE FOR FUCK'N GREENIES:

What did you think of that story? One man, 40 tons of fibreglass. One huge diesel engine thumping away through paradise! P.S. The dolphins were delicious!

SUPPLEMENTARY ANECDOTE:

I once owned a launch for two years that I used three times.

SUPPLEMENTARY, SUPPLEMENTARY ANECDOTE:

I once saw Dennis Conner in the supermarket. He bought tinned peaches.

POSSIBLE FACT:

Tinned peaches do not help you win the America's Cup.

LIST:

Reasons why, on a perfect day for boating, your boat is still in the marina:

1. You are working to pay the marina fee.
2. Your vessel is crawling with diesel engineers saying, 'Fuck, this looks bad!'
3. You are at your beach house in Omaha. Wanker!
4. Everyone in your family has told you that they honestly don't like boating.
5. You just can't be bothered untying the ropes. ('Sheets' if she is a yacht. Wanker.)
6. You have been told that two door latches are looking dodgy, and you can't face another bill.
7. You need to fill the tanks, and you only have a spare 18 grand on your eftpos card.
8. Your embroidered polo shirt is in the wash.
9. Your boat is for sale and you don't want to get her dirty.

ADDITIONAL FACT:

All boats are always for sale!

AMERICA'S CUP

What a stupid sport!

For decades it has been rendering itself down to the point it barely exists. The ultimate indictment of those who have had a hand in taking the America's Cup to the brink of oblivion is the fact that, after years off the water and after millions spent in courtrooms, only three teams put themselves forward to challenge. One of those teams was ill-prepared and missed most of their races. One other team refused to race until issues were sorted in court. Yes, some issues were still outstanding, even after the event started.

The true outrage for me is that I was an obsessive follower of the America's Cup. It was a truly outstanding event. If it were not for Team New Zealand, this regatta would be a complete joke. As it is, it's not quite complete in the laughable stakes. Watching these amazing pieces of plastic and dust fly over the water within the finest tolerances is a spectacle to behold, but how much better should it be? Oracle Team USA should be bloody ashamed of the way they have damaged this sport.

At the time of writing this, as was always going to be the case, Team New Zealand and Luna Rossa are into the Louis Vuitton Cup final. No surprises there. As Artemis did not have a boat for much of the regatta, it seemed unlikely they would win many races! I'm glad I don't know the final result, though, as it might distract me from my contempt of those who are destroying the sport.

The America's Cup should be about a challenging boat race, pitting vessels and sailors against each other. Rendering teams down to the ultimate challenge. Spectator boats should be jostling for position as supporters of numerous teams from many countries show their colours in triumph and defeat. But what is it? A courtroom drama so hard to follow it's almost lost me. God, I hope you lose, Oracle! You have almost plucked to death the goose that laid the golden eggs!

ANECDOTE:

One of the finest America's Cup moments for me was the end of a race on the Hauraki Gulf. Stars and Stripes were having a bastard of a regatta, but had just won against . . . I can't remember who. I was supporting them anyway, as I knew they couldn't beat us but I wanted to see them try. I also had a soft spot for Dennis Conner. (The only reason he was such an arse was his overbearing passion for the cup and yachting.) I had been out on the water in my boat watching, and as Stars and Stripes headed for home I saw dirty Dennis at the helm. I'm sure he waved. I know I did.

FACT:

New Zealand fell in love with the Luna Rossa team on the Hauraki Gulf. They were too good-looking to beat us, but we still wanted to look like them. They could out-class us in every way, but they would never chino their way to beating us at yachting!

STOP PRESS:
DJY 2013 SCOREBOARD:
WINNER LOUIS VUITTON CUP:- ETNZ
WINNER AMERICA'S CUP: - OTUSA

184

THE NEW ZEALAND HERALD

What a nasty, negative little rag *The New Zealand Herald* can be! Led by editor Shayne Currie, it is at times little better than a parish-pump newsletter on a large budget, gone tabloid. And that actually is my main gripe: it poses as a credible daily when in fact it is often nothing more than a shabby tabloid. This of course is just my opinion. And I may be wrong. But that's the guts of *The New Zealand Herald*: opinion, posing as fact. Often it is wrong or distorts the truth.

I dare say there are some decent human beings in its ranks, possibly with some talent, in fact I know there are. But at times, Shayne Currie and a troupe of performing hacks can fumble their way through the news of the day as they see fit. Thank God it's a dying medium if that is the best we have.

Posing as a media expert in the know, John Drinnan appears to say basically what he bloody well likes. On one occasion he contradicted a direct quote I had given another publication. I had said I turned down a job offer from TVNZ. Rather than looking at the possible ramifications of my rejecting this offer, he chose, as the expert in all this, to point people to the 'real' truth: quoting an unnamed insider, we were informed that this was not a job offer at all. I was merely on a list of possible candidates. For fuck's sake, I am in my fifties: I do know a job offer when I see one. Anyway, thanks John. You twat!

Brian Rudman is one of the many columnists employed by the *Herald* to pontificate on issues in lieu of actually reporting news. He can be entertaining and at times almost informative. But his comments about me at times have been spectacularly incorrect, according to a named source, Paul Henry. On one occasion he got things so wrong while pontificating on my clearly disastrous broadcasting ability that he appeared to contradict himself in the same missive. You see, when he's on a roll, he's on a roll and bugger reality. Another twat! In my opinion.

One of the saddest things is that many people do still believe what they read in the 'paper'. These people trust its news and facts rather than see it for what it is — theatre and speculation. More fool them. No — *Herald* fool them.

About their leader Shayne, I would say just this: I don't trust him. In fact, a phrase often used by a former broadcasting colleague of mine, Pam Corkery, whom I rate very highly, 'I wouldn't give him the steam off my piss', springs to mind.

SUPPLEMENTARY OPINION:

P erhaps the hardest job to do spectacularly well in a tabloid posing as a credible daily is that of gossip columnist. For years Rachel Glucina has excelled in her role with the *Herald*. Her column has expanded to become perhaps the whole honest point of the paper on the weekend, with supplementary reporting during the week. In a country as small as New Zealand, risking relationships with those you need on a weekly basis is a tightrope walk of extreme and continual peril. She has found a beautiful balance between confidante, best friend and bitch. She has coerced, blackmailed and bullied stories out of people with stunning finesse. Doing this job well is not so much about being liked as it is about being feared, and I know some pretty powerful people who have feared Rachel Glucina. In short, on a staff so packed with also-rans and hacks, Rachel shines brightly.

ANECDOTE:

On one occasion, in order to prove my standing as New Zealand's most racist inhabitant, *Herald* staff, reporters and a photographer invaded the private hamlet where I live and interviewed my neighbours. They also interviewed the proprietor of my local dairy. How excited must they have been to find so many races living immediately around me. Including some of the races I was reported in their own paper to be most offended by. You can just imagine the disappointment they must have felt on finding that these foreigners actually seemed happy to live in my vicinity. In fact some even liked me. Worse, they said I was nice to them. How would they report that?

Best to say nothing at all about it. After all, the facts should not be permitted to interfere with a *Herald* yarn. As luck would have it, after telling them repeatedly and politely to leave my private property and stop taking photographs on my land, I was forced to tell them repeatedly to fuck off, so they photographed me saying that and reported my outrage. Obviously without such key details as their repeatedly refusing to leave private property after being requested to do so. Instead, 'Paul Henry loses it!' Frankly, I am happy to tell them to fuck off anytime. It's just the way I roll. They had been on private property refusing to leave for so long I'd had time to personally speak on the phone with Shayne Currie. In spite of him fully understanding the facts of the matter, the story was nonetheless misrepresented on the front page. Style over substance.

OLIVE

My dear mother, Olive, is becoming more outrageous with every phone call she makes. Age is playing a wonderful game with her mind, and her ability to both frustrate and entertain increases daily. I am constantly stopped in the street by people inquiring after her, as a result of her brush with fame as my long-suffering mother. So, as well as displaying her prowess as an illustrator in this book, I will let you into her mind courtesy of the following transcript of a recent phone conversation with her.

The phone rings at my house:

P: Hello.

O: Who's this?

P: What do you mean, who's this? *(frustration begins)*

O: Who am I talking to?

P: What do you mean, who are you talking to? You rang me and I answered. Who the hell do you think I am? *(frustration already reaching fever pitch)*

O: Paul?

P: Yes, your son Paul.

O: What do you want? *(oh my God!)*

P: What do you mean, what do I want? *You* phoned *me!*

O: Who phoned you?

P: You!

O: Oh . . . Well . . . *(long pause as Mum rummages through what's left of her mind)* Yes. You know you were coming to see me Sunday? Well, I'm going to a Yorkshire day Sunday.

P: You are going to Yorkshire for the day. *(I have unwisely chosen to take the piss)*
O: Noooooo. *(27 seconds of hysterical laughter — she's back)* I AM GOING TO A YORKSHIRE DAY, STUPID!
P: Where's that, then?
O: Where's what? *(she's gone again)*
P: The fuck'n Yorkshire day. WHERE IS IT BEING HELD?
O: Oh. In . . . um . . . Oooh, you know . . . God . . . Oh, Papakura. *(what the fuck)*
P: Of course it is.
O: *(chuckles)*
P: So, I can't come and see you Sunday?
O: *(what happens now is a lengthy, real-time explanation*

of a completely unrelated yarn involving the dropping of a phone. Priceless!)
P: I said: does this all mean I can't come and visit you ON SUNDAY? *(I want out of this conversation, now)*
O: Oooh. Were you coming Sunday? I won't be here, I am doing a Yorkshire day.
P: Great, have a lovely day. You can tell me all about it when I see you.
O: When's that, then?

I can't begin to tell you how much more of this there is. Let's just leave it there.

FACT:

She had a great day in Yorkshire.

SUPPLEMENTARY FACT:

She is such a star. She makes me so proud.

SCIENTOLOGY

You freaks. You have got to be shitting me!

I am not prepared to give you the satisfaction of a full paragraph.

You are significantly more gullible than the Mormons, and dangerous, to boot!

Sweet baby Jesus, preserve me. Buddha, give me strength!

As something of a gift to the Scientologists reading this in order to warn off their clan, here is one of my mother's masterpieces. It is a picture of a cat, you gullible fools.

SEVEN SHARP

Seriously, is this the sum total of TVNZ's collective wisdom? What's it all about? Facile rubbish that might be okay in another time slot, but prime-time prestige current affairs? Not even close. The high ground was there for TVNZ to lose, and that's what they have done. Don't quote ratings. Just ask yourself, TVNZ: Am I proud of what I am producing for my money? Of course you're not! If something isn't working, you don't just throw more money and more staff at it. You suck it up and change it. In spite of the loss of face.

In the words of the famous sage Kenny Rogers: 'You gotta know when to hold 'em, gotta know when to fold 'em.' It's well past time to fold, *Seven Sharp*.

Don't blame the hosts — they must be desperate to be set free. The whole thing is so ill-conceived and badly-executed for that time slot. I could dissect it, but to do so would be akin to shooting fish in a barrel. The most challenged fool could chronicle the faults with this show.

NOTE TO TVNZ:

You don't actually need to reinvent the wheel (thank Christ), you just need to produce quality current affairs in a fresh way. Don't even begin to imagine that's what you are doing at 7pm now.

Your consultants should be shot. Don't wait until dawn.

ANECDOTE:

It's actually all my fault that it's so bad. I turned the job down, and what we have now is a rushed plan B. Should I say **sorry?** You're shitting me, aren't you?

SUPPLEMENTARY NOTE:

People who say, or said, that *Seven Sharp*'s disastrous performance is vindication for Mark Sainsbury, or that *Close Up* with Mark should have been retained, are fools. Replacing a disastrous show with one that is even worse is not vindication for the former. And it is certainly not an indication that the original show was actually good. The decision to replace *Close Up* with a completely revamped, cutting-edge show was long overdue. And still is.

STOP PRESS:
BOYD HAS PULLED THE PLUG:
DRINNAN SAYS I COULD BE
REPLACING HIM... TWAT!
NOTE TO TN3:
NO PLACE I'D RATHER BE!

115

THE GREAT GATSBY BY BAZ

Why? Just get the original out on Blu-ray, it's great — it's Gatsby. Typical Baz Luhrmann. Looks fantastic, but Baz we still need a yarn. The characters pissed me off, and I almost lost the will to live waiting for a storyline to develop. I started to feel the way I did watching that abysmal song-and-dance act in the hobbit house, as those short twats washed, dried and put the dishes away in real time. Shit, you owe me some heartbeats, Peter Jackson! It might be your trilogy, but it's my fuck'n life!

Why don't the Jacksons and the Luhrmanns of this world just sit down in front of the original *Wizard of Oz* and relearn how to tell a yarn?

NOTE TO BAZ:

No matter how beautiful you make it look, you still need to tell the yarn and it needs to be captivating. Don't waste any more of my precious life on your beautifully filmed puffery!

FOOTNOTE:

At this point in time I have not seen the film I starred in, in Hollywood. It could well be shit. Part of me is convinced it will be! But I know two things for sure: it has more storyline than it is humanly possible to follow in a short film, and there are no fuck'n hobbits.

WINSTON PETERS AND DEMOCRACY

At this point in time a rough look at averaging political polls would show that about 7 per cent of New Zealanders think Winston Peters is the best choice for prime minister of New Zealand. This fact alone proves democracy is hugely flawed. As if we needed proof. Any system that gives stupid and disengaged fools as much influence as the intelligent and interested is dangerously open to distortion. Or, in other words: dangerously open to Winston Peters.

With the first-past-the-post system of voting that New Zealand used for much of our political history, you required many more stupid people to tick lunacy before it impacted on society directly; now, under mixed-member-proportional, the odds are in stupid people's hands. We are reaping the rewards of that now. So is Winston Peters. We are also breeding more stupid and disengaged voters, so the future looks bright for Winston and his ilk.

So why am I singling out Winston Peters when surely there are more deserving political opportunists to slag off? Well, the answer to that is simple: because Winston is the most dangerous. He is one of the cleverest. He has almost as much political cunning as Helen Clark. But the talent he possesses above his political talent is charm. In an almost charmless crowd, Winston stands tall. (In reality he is quite short.) I have seen detractors melt in his sight. I have seen detractors offer him good, helpful advice in a way they would not with any other politician. He gains followers in spite of the fact many know they are being squired over a cliff.

So, back to the facts at hand. After decades as a politician, a minister of the Crown, and a party leader, what has Winston actually done that is positive? There is the Gold Card for seniors and — oh God, that's right — without Winston we would not be reaping the benefits of Brendan Horan's extensive talents.

Winston would have us believe that he brings honesty and perhaps some transparency to politics, but in reality he is an expert at queering the pitch. It is that expertise that has the prime minister conceding he would do a deal with Winston, even though he has always said he would not. John Key needs to be aware that in any deal with Winston it's not likely to be Winston who suffers the slings and arrows of outrageous fortune.

So does Winston outrage me? Not one bit. I take my hat off to the man. He's a star, albeit so tarnished that he hardly shines at all now.

It is the 7 per cent who outrage me. And bloody democracy!

House of Representatives? My God, we've got some duffers in parliament. And far too many of them. When I bemoan this fact with acquaintances, they will often say, 'But it is a house of representatives, so they should represent all facets of life.' This argument is used by fools who don't understand the meaning of what they say.

On the surface their argument is correct: our group of representatives needs to represent everyone. But they are suggesting we need fools to represent fools. Maori to represent Maori. Women to represent women. For fuck's sake. Well, what about poor criminals? Surely they should be represented by criminals? And the sick? Should they be represented by the well? I think not. By doctors? Certainly not. We should go out of our way to hunt down very unwell people to represent them. Just as we need at least one complete lunatic to represent the truly insane. I know, we do have John Banks, but he can't be everywhere! The fact is, we are over-governed partly because fools want to see people who look like them in parliament.

VOTING TEST:

Why, when a voting test is suggested, is it ridiculed out of hand? Perhaps because the chance it will be adopted is so slim. Perhaps because, with every breeding cycle in New Zealand, more people who will never be able to pass are produced. Perhaps because, if it were, Peter Dunne would email you the answers in advance! Perhaps! Oh, for heaven's sake, he would never do that.

If you have no interest in voting and have taken no steps to learn the most basic details of our voting system or the platforms that parties and candidates stand on, surely your vote should not count?

The ballot should begin with three simple politically-based multi-choice questions. To fail just one would invalidate your vote.

An example of the sort of questions would be:

1. Does New Zealand have a: (A) president; or (B) prime minister?
2. Is New Zealand's voting system currently: (A) STV; (B) FPP; or (C) MMP?
3. How old do you have to be to vote in New Zealand? (A) 21; (B) 18; or (C) 16?

Yes, I know, simplistic. But you would be amazed, and I hope shocked, at how many voters could not answer all three questions. After all, so many people still don't understand MMP.

Perhaps a bonus vote should be given to those at the other end of the spectrum who can answer three tricky political questions, or who have bought a copy of my book!

QUESTIONS:

Should the Electoral Commission put so much effort into getting people to enrol? Should they allow late enrolments? Should they use any language other than English and Maori? If New Zealanders eligible to enrol don't understand deadlines, they are either not interested or too stupid or both. If you can't understand the English or Maori language, should you be eligible to enrol?

FOR BUYING MY BOOK YOU GET
AN EXTRA VOTE...
PRESENT THIS VOUCHER TO THE
RETURNING OFFICER AT YOUR
POLLING BOOTH...

HELLO. MY NAME IS: _____
OF: _____ ELECTORATE:
I VOTE NATIONAL AND GET
ONE EXTRA VOTE BY ORDER
OF: _____ PAUL HENRY AUTHOR

120

TOP NINE GROUPS OF PEOPLE WHO OUTRAGE ME

1. People who think Winston Peters should be New Zealand's next prime minister.
2. People who think they are special because they are disabled, deformed or disfigured. They are just people!
3. People who live courtesy of the taxpayer and show no gratitude.
4. People whose political beliefs are so one-sided that they are blinded to the fact that opposing parties do have good ideas.
5. People who steal the magic from children's eyes.
6. People who drive with disregard for others. It's fuck'n arrogant.
7. Closed-minded people.
8. People who stop walking in front of people who hadn't intended to stop.
9. Socialists and all who support the concept of bleeding a part of society so that others might get a free transfusion.

DESIGNATED PARKING

I have no idea how the calculation for disabled car parks versus able-bodied works. What I do know is that the extraordinarily well-placed disabled car parks are often empty when the rest of the car park is full. It seems unreasonable that an able-bodied person gets wet because they have had to walk two kilometres in the rain from the vacant park they found, and just before they reach the mall doors they come across four empty disabled parks. Those parks are waiting for disabled people who have obviously decided to stay home because of the rain. How stupid is that? You have to feel sorry for the able-bodied: they get wet while disabled people sit in front of their TVs at home.

There are just too many of these 'special' parking spaces. However, the parking spaces that really outrage me are the old people and the mothers with prams/toddlers parks.

Most old people who drive are completely capable of walking, so do them a favour and make them walk greater distances for exercise. If malls and supermarkets are determined to have designated car parks for the old, put them as far from the doors as possible. Rename them 'move-it-or-lose-it parks'.

As for those with young children: your decision to have them, not mine! Why should you also get the best parks? It is so unreasonable that fit young breeders should get preference over me. You are probably much more capable of struggling with your appallingly behaved child and a pram than I am struggling with my brilliance.

And when you do make it inside, your child screams and fits like a banshee, further victimising me. Maybe you should have designated shops, too, so I never have to compromise my life so that you can further your animalistic motivation to breed.

123

What's next? Designated car parks for the very stupid? For those who are unable to find their way to the front doors unless they can see them?

THOUGHT:

How about a designated area for people who have cars valued at over $80,000? A sort of executive area, with wider parking spaces and carpet, all under cover. Cordoned off with gold-coloured bollards and red velvet rope. Perhaps a travelator that bypasses Kmart, delivering you straight to Peter Alexander so you can pick up another pair of $120 sleeping shorts!

How about luxury car parks for those who pay over $100,000 per year in tax? Yes, they might be rich, but they paid for the road that leads to the car park, and for your maternity leave, so it would be a nice way of saying thank you.

EXECUTIVE SUMMARY:

There are just too many 'designated' car parks. Reduce the number. Or ditch the idea completely. Alternatively, have a designated car park right by the front door of every mall, supermarket, bank, etc, for 'Paul Henry'.

124

AUTHOR'S OBSERVATION:

In the States, the car parks are much bigger. It's fantastic. This is for two reasons. First, everyone in the States is disabled. And secondly, most Americans appreciate the need, as I do, to drive enormous vehicles that at least appear to be able to survive a nuclear attack.

125

PUBLIC HOLIDAY SURCHARGES

How have we let this happen? New Zealand is dependent to a significant extent on tourism and travel. It was a global haven from extra taxes, tipping and surcharges. But no longer. First there was GST, a tax I reluctantly support as a result of its comparative fairness and the flexibility it gives the individual. GST is also fixed in the price of retail sales, so is not a sneaky add-on designed to fool customers ripe for the picking. The public holiday surcharge is an invidious tax placed on sales and service by nasty little businesses taking advantage of a gullible and passive marketplace. Some bigger businesses are starting to adopt the surcharge, too, as they see that it is now accepted as part of our way of life.

So back to my question: how have we let this happen? Through **quiet acceptance.** It's as though as a nation we are saying, 'I'm bending over — insert your surcharge here!'

Seeing minor protest to the nasty surcharge, some reactive businesses signposted the fact that they were surcharge-free, but blind fools continued to flock to the surcharge-chargers, so what's the point? There was even vocal support for those charging it, with customers expounding the right of business owners to recoup the extra cost of salaries. What an outrage! Public holidays are boon times for many businesses; they open because there is money to be made. *Extra* money in many cases. If they can't afford to pay wages, take the fuck'n day off. Close!

You might say to me, as many have, that if I don't want to pay a surcharge I can choose not to frequent those that charge it. Believe you me, I do! At times to my complete inconvenience. Those businesses are missing out on my spending. But if more people had said no to surcharges, they would not exist, and our country would be better for it.

I have seen surcharges of over 20 per cent being applied, with queues of people entering the premises. Rabid overcharging! Profiteering bastards! And foolish twats supporting them!

If **McDonald's** doesn't need a surcharge, why does anyone?

It might not be too late, but knowing New Zealanders as I do, it probably is. And bend . . .

CALL TO ACTION:

Condemn all businesses which charge public holiday surcharges by boycotting them on public holidays and perhaps at all times. Stand up straight and support those which don't charge them, and make your reasons known.

ANECDOTE:

I found myself in Rotorua on a public holiday. Everywhere, small businesses run by nasty small-minded people were charging a surcharge to queues of customers happy to be ripped off. Not service stations, not dairies. They still have staff to pay, but magically they manage to do it without charging extra. I saw a

sign at **Rebel Sport:** *40% off everything.* How can that be? No surcharge and 40 per cent off? Is it creative accounting? No, it's good business.

FILL OUT YOUR OWN LIST OF
PUBLIC HOLIDAY SURCHARGE
BASTARDS!

NAME:

1/

2/

3/

4/

5/

6/

7/

COCA-COLA

Dateline: July 2013, and, after decades of ignoring the increasingly alarming health trends in society, Coca-Cola has decided to admit to being part of the obesity problem. This manifests as something of a marketing campaign, presumably designed, as all good marketing campaigns are, to sell more product. All of a sudden the CEO is available for live interviews regarding society's alarming trend to obesity and the soft drink's obviously injurious links to it. 'Yes, we use a shit-load of sugar . . . but we have products that are sugar-free. Yes, we sell family-sized packs large enough to bathe in . . . but we have small bottles, too. Yes, we are linked to fatties . . . but we want to be linked to sporty types.'

You see, Coca-Cola has come up with a ridiculous plan, which the CEO can't fully explain, to rid the company of any guilt and to fill the minds of the increasingly fat with good thoughts about the product. This will, it must be hoped by Coca-Cola, see sales skyrocket.

This is such an unwise strategy for a company like Coke. Not because its CEO was such a poor performer when it came to fronting it, but because it is a huge admission that plays right into the hands of the company's key detractors. These people, such as the 'stop obesity' campaigners, just want Coke shut down. They want extra taxes on products like sugar-rich soft drinks, and in their quiet moments probably dream of taking part in lynching mobs that end with the Coke CEO's corpse being cut down from the tree and dowsed in the last bottle of his product to survive the great anti-sugar uprising.

So Coke, here is what your PR and advertising masterminds should have told you: 'These people will not be won over, so don't engage with them.'

It is Coke's responsibility to return as much profit as possible to the stakeholders. It's not Coke's responsibility to fix a society coming apart at the seams as a result of people with the freedom to choose making the wrong choices for themselves and their children.

NOTE TO PARENTS:

If you are watching yourself and your children grow fat and unhealthy and are filling your shopping cart with Coke and similar products, if you are sending your children to school with a Coke a day and feeding it to your infants, then you are guilty of child abuse. You are a complete fuckwit and should be loudly condemned by society. You don't need to be educated — you need to be ashamed of yourself. You are doing this: there is no one else to blame but you. Sort it out, for your children's sake!

NOTE TO OBESITY CAMPAIGNERS:

Don't pussyfoot around this issue anymore. It is not society in general that is at fault: point the finger to those responsible. The fools drinking and eating themselves into obesity. The abusive parents feeding convenience foods in huge quantities to their children. Why? Because they are convenient. They don't need anyone else to take responsibility for this — they need to be told to take responsibility for it themselves. Read them the fuck'n Riot Act!

NOTE TO COKE:

Sell as much as you can, to make as much money as you can. If that means you need to find a new PR and marketing team, or even a new CEO, do it now. That's *your* job.

AUTHOR'S PREDICTION:

Coke-free zones. Tax on Coke. Appalling anti-Coke advertisements, using *Shortland Street* actors and former All Blacks or current netball players giving testimonials on their Coke-free lives. Worse still, a chubby middle-aged Maori woman speaking in thoughtful tones, holding a photograph of her deceased mother: 'Yup . . . She passed away because of "the Cokes"!'

131

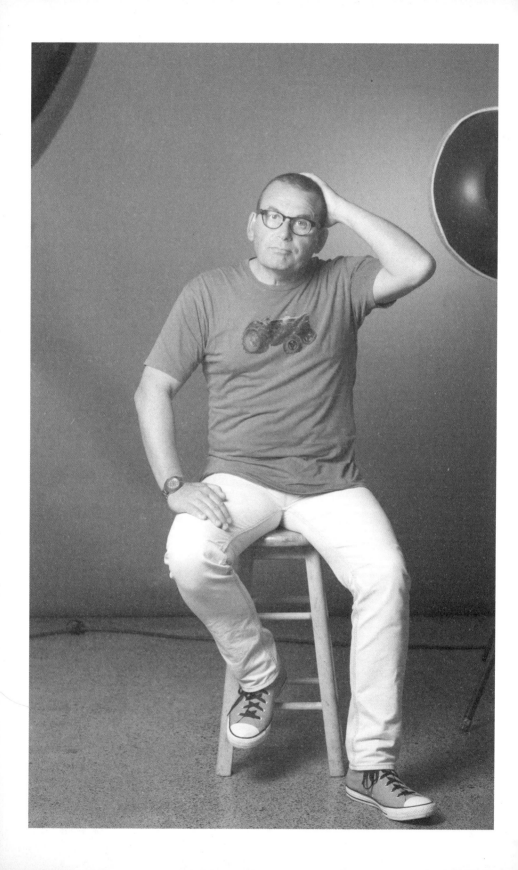

CULTURAL SENSITIVITY V HEALTH AND SAFETY

A number of years ago I was visiting a relative in hospital. It was a large provincial hospital in the lower North Island. He was very sick, as were the other patients on the ward.

When I turned the corner in the corridor from the lift to the ward, I could see a large, noisy family lying on the floor and basically blocking my path. They were eating, laughing, and just generally behaving as though they were at home in the front garden having a party. Their young children were running around unrestrained. These arrogant arseholes were thoughtlessly causing added angst to the staff, patients and other visitors there.

It was unbelievable that this large Maori family could not give a damn for the feelings of others. But worse still was the attitude of hospital management, who had clearly given the green light to this behaviour on the basis that it was 'culturally sensitive' to do so. That is nothing short of offensive bullshit. Cultural sensitivity, my arse! These people were showing no sensitivity to others, and deserved none shown to them. The door was all they should have been shown.

Hospitals are not for Maoris; they are not for any particular race. Hospitals are for the sick. And as such they should have their own set of codes and acceptable behaviour. It is cowardly political correctness of the worst kind that leads to hospitals' acceptance of this kind of thing. It is also counter-productive to recuperation. Surely the hospital environment should be made as stress-free as possible? So in

accepting this behaviour, hospital management are compromising health and creating an even more challenging environment for staff and patients. Cowards. Bloody cowards.

I know this is not an isolated case, as I have on several occasions seen common areas and TV rooms completely overwhelmed by extended families basically living in hospitals. Fuck cultural sensitivity in such circumstances. God, most circumstances!

NOTE TO DHBS:

See if you can source a backbone and have it installed as soon as possible.

NOTE TO MAORI AND OTHER RACES THAT SEE THEMSELVES AS 'SPECIAL':

If you want treatment at one of our fine public health facilities, at the hands of the best Indian and Chinese medical professionals we can muster, remember this: it is not about you at all. It is about mending people and helping them cope with shit. Show respect to others and they will hopefully show respect to you. Do not intimidate others. Intimidation is the tool of the very stupid and socially corrupt.

NOTE TO WARD STAFF:

Print copies of this chapter, laminate them and post them on the wards. Just don't let anyone catch you doing it — hospitals are full of socialist sympathisers.

NOTE TO READER:

This book would make an excellent gift for those in hospital, both patients and staff. Not your copy; it will get covered in germs. Purchase supplementary copies.

POSSIBLE FACT:

After reading this book, 100 per cent of patients recuperate 34 times faster than they would otherwise.

DIETING

For God's sake, it's not rocket science, is it? The proliferation of diet books is even more outrageous than that of cookbooks. You don't need any diet books. None.

The fuck'n grapefruit diet? Give me strength. Atkins? Jesus Christ!

Ask yourself this: do I want to make someone else rich? Do I need another distraction from my need to lose weight? Why, if they work, are there so many diets and books and classes? Why, if any of it works, are there so many fatties?

Here's the thing. You are fat because you eat too much and don't move enough. You will lose weight if you eat a bit less and move a bit more. Sorted!

It is a fuck'n outrage how many people compromise their enjoyment of life because they are on some charlatan's diet. Grow up and lose weight. Then enjoy your life a bit more. Stop fuck'n making excuses and boring others shitless with your tales

of **woe and fattiness.** Stop making excuses for yourself. If you are fat and you are running your own life, get up onto your knees and sort it out. You are a burden on others and yourself. If you are not running your own life and someone else is making you fat, poison them, eat less and run like the wind.

NOTE:

If you are fat or overweight and you are okay with it, if you are not constantly on diets, purchasing diet products, making others rich off your despair, or sucking the life blood out of those around you with your disastrous life choices . . . good for you. Nothing wrong with a bit of extra weight. If you're fat and you love it, clap your hands. And if you're too fat to clap your hands, have your nurse clap for you.

FACT:

Fat people who vote Labour are 63 per cent less likely to lose any weight than fat people who vote National.

ADDITIONAL FACT:

The person who cares the most about your weight is the person you are paying to help you lose it. Just like all lawyers, if things are going badly for you, it's payday for them!

AUTHOR'S TOP NINE TIPS FOR LOSING WEIGHT:

1. Eat less.
2. Eat less.
3. Eat less.
4. Eat less.
5. Eat less.
6. Eat less.
7. Eat less.
8. Eat less.
9. Move more.

DRIVING

Driving: it's the great social leveller. We have to mingle. The rich, the poor. The good, the bad and the ugly are shoulder to shoulder. The competent and complete morons are no more than inches apart — if you're lucky!

Now let me be quite clear, up-front. I don't want to share the roads with anyone at all. So the current situation is completely unacceptable. It is quite simply . . . an outrage.

To be honest, I am not a perfect driver. I very occasionally find myself in the wrong lane. And I very often drive too fast. When these things happen, I expertly and courteously handle the situation. If only that could be said about others.

I am constantly frustrated by the effort that goes into enforcing the speed limit when there are thousands of people driving arrogantly and dangerously at all speeds. Yes, speed kills — but so does complete fuck'n incompetence. Get those bastards before I am forced to take up arms against them. You don't have much time, **I am close to breaking point!**

I reluctantly accept that there are many different people driving with many different motivations and social distractions. For me, though, when you are driving that has to be the thing. You might have a child screaming in the back, but, fuck it, at that moment you are a driver not a mother. You might have just lost your job, but you are driving, so that doesn't matter. You might be Asian, but try to concentrate . . . Fuck'n concentrate on driving! I love cars almost as much as I love boats. And almost as much as I hate people. So obviously I detest those who fumble through the process of motoring just as they fumble through life. I have heard many people bemoan the fact you can have children without a licence but you can't drive without a licence. God, some of those who have managed to secure a driver's licence could never manoeuvre their private parts into such tight, dark places to ever procreate. Thank Christ!

THE MOST FUCK'N ANNOYING THINGS MORONS ARE DOING ON MY ROADS:

So, here it is. An incomplete list of the most fuck'n annoying things morons are doing on my roads. In no particular order.

Braking on the motorway: The motorway is not for braking. The only reason to brake on a motorway is to avoid a collision. You don't brake to change lanes; you indicate and drive into gaps. You don't brake because you have missed something or seen something or for any random reason. It is alarmingly easy to cause accidents on the motorway, and a set of brake lights can be all it takes. A set of brake lights and a moron behind the wheel.

Speeding up when there is a passing lane: It is a passing lane designed for passing. You know there is a car or two behind you, so why do you speed up when there is a passing lane? If this is you — you are an arse of the highest order! Much effort has been put into studying why some drivers do this, and a consensus view is that bad drivers feel more at ease increasing speed when the road width increases. Bad drivers — yes, that's you, a bad driver who should be forced off the road by penalties so harsh that you have to sell your vehicle to pay the fine. If you are a slow driver, fair enough. Just don't slow others down. Be considerate of those who don't want to waste their lives behind you.

Asian drivers: Okay, so maybe not all Asian drivers, just most. If I see someone doing the things on this list in Auckland, I automatically think they must be Asian, and when I see they are not, I am surprised. Why? Is it because I am racist? No. It's because when I see drivers doing many of the things on this list, chances are they are Asian. Fact, not racism! Often highly educated, often good with money and business. Generally better at life than non-Asians — so why are they pains in the arse on the road?

Uneven speeds: So you are involved in a conversation. Maybe texting or just enjoying your own brand of mindlessness. Whatever it is, it is making you change speed. Slow to fast . . . to slow . . . I just don't want to be on the road with you. Concentrate on driving or stay indoors!

Driving slowly in the fast lane: I have been told it is not the fast lane at all, but the overtaking lane. Whatever it is, it is where I like to be, because I drive fast. I hate those who stay in the fast lane as others overtake them to their left. You are going too slowly: shift or be shifted. Do these people think it is their job to act as a sort of rolling blockade to slow me down? Live your

life in the slow lane if you want, but stay out of my life. **Move over, I'm coming through!**

Lane-hoppers: You cause accidents. You drive in an unsafe way at speed and should be stopped. The only excuse for this behaviour is avoiding slow twats in the fast lane!

Campervans: If you can't drive at the speed limit, or confine yourself to the hours of 2.30am to 4am, stay off my road. I can't believe how inconsiderate some of these road maggots are. There are rules regarding pulling over, if only you knew them. Remember, it's your holiday not mine. Keep it to yourself, you feral, bohemian pensioner.

Not knowing where you are or want to be: *You* are lost, not the poor people forced to share the road with you. Pull well off the road and call for help. Actually just pull well off the road. Do not slow down and peer in all directions. Do not mindlessly change speed and direction, oblivious to others. Your bewilderment translates as arrogant stupidity.

Changing lanes to avoid queues of traffic: Oh, this is a goodie. You should be locked up, you arsehole! So others are queuing for a turn-off or motorway entrance and you purposely drive in the wrong adjacent lane, until the last minute, and then force your way in. So you think you are better than everyone else, your time is more important. You fuck'n arsehole. But worse than you are the little shits who let you in. Cowardly little shits who smile at you and leave a gap. I despise you all. Including those who leave gaps in front of them in the queue just big enough for these shits to slimy their way in. When you let these morons in, you are extending the queue for everyone behind you as well. And we are the nice ones. Shoot these people.

Not indicating: I passed my driving test in England. My driving instructor said to me, 'Always remember this — it doesn't matter how badly you are doing something, so long as you make it perfectly clear to others what it is you are trying to do.' He also had this **pearl of wisdom:** 'You will never get into trouble on the road if you never do anything that causes anyone else to either slow down or change direction.' Not perfect, but pretty good advice. Clearly unknown to many. Indicate. And indicate in time. Don't brake then indicate, or slow and turn and indicate, you halfwit! If you do this, know this: I detest you! You have no right to be on the road with such an arrogant attitude.

Parking like a dick: If it is not an angle park, don't park on an angle. Park in the centre of your park. I get so annoyed at inconsiderate shits who take up more than their park as a result of their negligent parking. They should instantly be towed at huge personal expense. I have tolerance, however, for those who take up a great deal of space because they drive large vehicles, as long as they have parked well. If it is overlapping due to size, that's okay!

ADDITIONAL ROAD-RELATED ANNOYANCES:

Road-work signs: Who polices these? I can't count the number of times I am forced to slow to a crawl only to find that the work hasn't started, or that they have packed up for summer or are working 10 kilometres up the road. Basically, there is no need to slow down. This is time-wasting and dangerous in itself. It is crying wolf and training me and others to believe it is not necessary to slow down. The works companies should be fined for distracting motorists unnecessarily. Shit, it is so frustrating to lose momentum.

Roundabouts: The only way you can legally drive around a roundabout in New Zealand is to the right. So why do we have to indicate right? It is just another thing to get wrong. At roundabouts you should only have to indicate left to exit.

Simple. If you are not indicating to the left, you are staying on. Don't make things hard for these morons. If it is compulsory to turn right, surely to indicate right is redundant?

Safer speed zones: So that's it, is it? You have given up on policing the road and have decided to take us back to the horse-and-cart days of driving slowly. What's next? A man holding a red flag walking in front of our cars? That, to be fair, would cut the accident rate down. I totally oppose turning the 100km speed limit into a 90km limit as has happened on much of State Highway 27, just because morons can't drive safely. Just another example of me being criminalised for the incompetence of others.

PERSONAL ANECDOTE:

I am driving the Mustang between Las Vegas and Barstow. The traffic is very heavy in all four lanes. Speed limit is 75 miles an hour, but like the rest of the traffic in the fast lane I am hovering around the 85 mile an hour mark. The trucks know their place. It is wherever they want to be, and they keep up with the rest of the traffic or lead it. If not, they pull over, just like the Winnebagos. (Like that would ever happen in New Zealand!) I see a huge cloud of black smoke on the horizon that gets closer quickly at 85 miles an hour. When alongside, I see it is almost the eighth wonder of the world. A ferocious desert scrub fire fanned by baking-hot winds. Massive and fascinating. But all viewed at 85 miles an hour. (God bless America!) Yes, they are not unheard of, but also not commonly seen at close proximity. Yes, sometimes American drivers do rubberneck, but only for multiple shootings. For the most part, drivers in many other countries manage not to allow a paper bag at the side of the motorway to slow them to a crawl and force a multi-lane traffic jam. Whereas in New Zealand a touch of rain creates gridlock.

CONCLUSION:

Let's just say this. Driving is a considerable responsibility. Maybe you don't understand the passion and drama of motoring. And maybe you never will. Maybe you will spend your motoring days locked in a hideous Nissan something or Toyota another. Maybe you will be boxed into a fuck'n Daihatsu your whole driving life or silently simpering along in a bloody hybrid. Whatever. Stay out of my way and stay away from those who, like me, love to drive and drive well. In short: know your place.

NINE GREAT COMMON CAR NAMES:

1. Jeep Patriot
2. Ford Raptor
3. Dodge Ram
4. Ford Explorer
5. Ford Mustang
6. Aston Martin Vanquish
7. Chevrolet Silverado
8. Holden Volt
9. Isuzu Mysterious Utility

NINE FRIGHTFUL COMMON CAR NAMES:

1. Mazda Bongo Wagon
2. Nissan Liberty
3. Porsche Cayenne
4. Nissan Sylphy
5. Suzuki Super Carry
6. Toyota Vitz
7. Kia Sephia
8. Hyundai Grandeur
9. Nissan Cedric

Ford in general have selected names successfully. There are so many like the Ranger, Bronco and Territory. Nissan do spectacularly well in the terrible name stakes. BMW, Mercedes and some others have been classy and safe, just using serial numbers and letters.

My suggestions to Nissan and Ford for some new car names:

- Nissan Macramé
- Nissan Cystitis
- Nissan Buffet
- Nissan à la Carte
- Nissan Pancreas
- Ford Survivor
- Ford Eradicator
- Ford Enterprise

FEMINISM

The concepts of feminism, sexual equality and women's rights are now (thank Christ) so out of date that it would be foolish for me to include a mention of them in this book. I do it here just to reinforce the fact that I did not overlook the topic!

Just as any department for women's affairs should be closed down and any reference to glass ceilings scratched from the record, so the whole topic should be consigned to history. It was a diabolical uprising that almost completely destroyed the ability most pretty little ladies had to craft the perfect pavlova.

LIST:

I am so tempted to list here the names of offensive man-like women I have been forced to engage with in the past on the basis that it is only fair to give them a leg-up. But I am still in the lengthy process of forgiveness, so I will instead leave a blank form for male readers to insert the names associated with their horrific memories, and for female readers to list the names of those who tried to recruit them to the dark side.

YOUR LIST OF HE-LADIES...

NAME:	SCORE:

Note: Pretty Scale: 1 = your butcher; 10 = Lorraine Downes.

149

GAY MARRIAGE

As I write this, I am watching live on television two lesbians getting married in the Rotorua Museum. Surprisingly, they are both quite pretty and both in wedding gowns. (Shouldn't one be in a suit?) Incidentally, the building is much less magnificent on the inside than it is outside.

Before I continue, I need to stress that, although I am not myself a lesbian, I do have a very good understanding of lesbianism. In fact, I completely understand the attraction — to the point that I think some of the same things they do every 20 seconds or so.

If you have become aroused, just take a moment to calm down, or alternatively just take a moment.

Pause for arousal to subside.

Right. The reason this wedding is live on TV is that it is day one of same-sex marriage in New Zealand, and men and men, and women and women, are getting married like there is no tomorrow. That doesn't bother me at all. In fact I find it entertaining as a novelty, but, just like marriage itself, the novelty will wear off, and no doubt in some cases lead to same-sex divorce. Poetic justice for those who want this weird sort of fairness. Call the same-sex lawyers now!

It is weird because marriage is a tradition. It is for a man and a lady to partake in. Although I don't care, I do have sympathy for those who do, as it is their beliefs that the gays are trampling on. I am fully supportive of the same legal protection being afforded homosexual couples as it is married heterosexuals, but an apple is an apple, and marriage is for apples, you bloody oranges.

Anyway, it is time for another couple of oranges to tie the knot in Rotorua. Oh fuck — they're both men! That *can't* be right!

INVINCIBLE CYCLISTS AND GYM-GOERS

It is poncey Lycra not manly Kevlar, you arrogant fools! When you spill euphorically out of the gym and launch yourselves into the path of oncoming cars, what, if anything, is going on in your minds? You are not closer to God because you exercise, you know. But you *can* be closer to God if you get in my way! I have so far managed to avoid the extraordinarily attractive temptation to bowl you over outside Les Mills on Victoria Street. It is dark and you just blunder over the road between cars because you presumably think you own the place, you're so holy. Oh, you exercise! Pardon me! One day I am going to go apeshit. Ape-fuck'n-shit!

I expect you are heading over to some bike rack to unlock your fancy cycle so that you can continue to pollute the roads with your arrogant disregard for the motorists who are paying their way. Go on: ride three abreast. Shake your fist at the poor bugger who can only just fit between you and oncoming traffic in his Hummer. Be the arse you are, and then click-clack your way into a café with your stupid bike shoes and stink up the place with your whiffy Lycra shorts, displaying the outline of your half-crushed uncircumcised man's penis.

Cyclist

POSSIBLE FACT:

C ircumcised men do not ride bikes.

PERSONAL:

I used to have a bike. Then I grew up.

LAS VEGAS / NEW YORK

I take an instant dislike to prissy, pious people who rubbish Las Vegas offhand. Most have never been there. Well, news for you: Las Vegas doesn't give a shit about you and is better for your non-attendance. I have lost count of the number of times people have condemned Las Vegas when I have talked about it being one of my favourite places. 'It's so wasteful, so garish, so fake . . .' God, just listen to yourselves. Without exception the people who hold these views are pains in the arse!

The fact is, Las Vegas could teach the world how to recycle if it could be bothered, but I love that it can't. It's brash because it knows it has nothing to be ashamed of, and, so far as being fake, it is about as original as anything comes. The brilliance of creating a slice of Egypt that isn't full of bloody Egyptians is only surpassed by the stunning genius of creating a replica of Paris without the ghastly French.

It is impossible to count the true wonders of the world that have been created in Vegas, but that's the thing: Vegas *is* the wonder. It's under threat, though. The threat comes from the pious wowsers who don't understand, as Vegas does, that we humans run the planet and have every right to put a great deal of effort into our own entertainment. Every time I go there — and it's often — yet another energy-efficient-bloody-bulb has replaced a beautiful incandescent bulb. And now the dopey fools at MGM Grand have given in to the animal-activist Nazis and ditched the lions in the glass cage. Damn you all. Those lions were treated like kings.

Most of Las Vegas's detractors, I have found, are also inclined to praise New York and condemn Los Angeles. I love Los Angeles, but it doesn't need my endorsement, so enough about that.

155

It's the poncey twats who sing the praises of New York whom I can't stand. 'Oh, the art galleries, the theatre!' Not only does LA have that and more, Las Vegas *is* an art gallery and theatre. Obviously the social snobs who hail New York overlook the fact that it is quite literally a shit-hole. Too many people in too small a space. Too cold in winter, and far too hot in summer. The people are oppressed by the very architecture, let alone each other. The underground is like a soup made from human excrement, and over-ground can at times be worse. New York is no more than a great long weekend and a great sandwich. I won't be going back until they get a huge glass bowl full of lions and install them in the lobby of the Empire State Building.

SUPPLEMENTARY FACT:

I f you are one of those who condemn the entire United States out-of-hand, as many do, it's possible you have no idea how stupid you are. Let me tell you. 'Very' is the answer!

LIST:

I love the USA in spite of its many faults — and *because* of others. I have enough anecdotes to fill a book, but rather than recount them, I gift you a short list of some stunning US mini adventures you can easily have.

1. One-day road trip: Pacific Coast Highway from San Francisco to Carmel. Make sure you stay on the PCH all the way. Take it slowly and stop often. It could just challenge your view that New Zealand has the best vistas in the world. Take a long look at the sea lions.

2. Two- to three-day road trip: Las Vegas to San Fran, staying at Mammoth. On day two, fill up with cheaper petrol just over the Nevada border. You'll see where!

3. Have your photo taken between the enormous legs of the Marilyn Monroe statue in Palm Springs. (Sadly, she is wearing knickers.) Walk in the footsteps of the true Legends of the Silver Screen.

4 Visit Salvation Mountain just out of Niland, next to the Salton Sea. It is a monument to the significance of the individual. A loud voice from those who could so easily have no voice: the ordinary man. While you are there, look down on Slab City, where the ordinary come to rest.

5 Drive over London Bridge in Lake Havasu City, Arizona. It's a monument to all that is the American Dream.

6 Visit the town of Chloride in Arizona and have a bowl of chilli in the old stage-coach inn. Can't remember the name of the place, but it's just off the main shopping road. The town has fewer than 400 residents, so it isn't hard to find. On the way out, visit the cemetery. Don't stay after dark.

7 Just do a whole day on Route 66. Try Kingman to Flagstaff. Take it slow. Drive an American car and listen to American sixties and seventies music. Stop at a diner and have a pickle and coffee.

8 Drive another 45 minutes up the freeway from Flagstaff and visit Meteor Crater. It could blow your mind. We really are just a speck on the backside of insignificance. The crater doesn't need America to sing its size. It's just quite big. If there is time, go stand on a corner in Winslow, Arizona. You might see a fine sight.

9 Go to Las Vegas. See either 'O' or 'KÀ' — get good seats. And do a helicopter trip into the Grand Canyon. Natural wonders mixing with the man-made. Fantastic!

What I have cleverly done (and pretty much everything I do is clever) is suggest a pile of things you could do on a two-week trip if you wanted. There are more 'amazing places' in the States by a

159

country mile, but after you have done the above your appetite for more will get you to them.

My biggest tip is this: rent a car, and go your own way.

MOTEL
66
ROUTE 66
Welcome to KINGMAN
CLEANROOMS AC PHONE
CABLE TV POOL WI-FI
3BEDS XTRA 27 95 36 95
TRUCKS OK
VACANCY

Salvation Mountain.

Meteor Crater.

Political bunker, Canberra.

Paul Henry stands alongside the bastion of our
great land. She's taller than you might think.

POLITICS

In politics, like some other endeavours, your achievements are singular, your failures cumulative. It is a matter of achieving as much as you can while you can. Once you have accumulated enough failures, real or imagined, it is time to go. Recognising that and acting on it depends on what type of person you are and what motivates you. It is somewhat easier to recognise the almost total rejection that comes with failure if you have made it to prime minister, which is why ex-PMs almost always move on faster.

The Jonathan Hunt brigade is there for the long haul, though. Although I don't want to speak ill of the dead — what? God, he's alive! Anyway, these are the people motivated by the challenge to avoid ever being thrown out. They want 'in' for all their working lives if they can. Murray McCully has become one. A sort of partly-reliable mild wind under the wings of whoever looks to be Murray's best bet. Peter Dunne is a better example. He carries his loyalties with his principles in a bag he's prepared to set down on any desk. It has been a long political career with only a very few magnificent moments. He is well past his use-by date, and has well missed the chance to leave with dignity intact. However, he is a success in the longevity stakes, and has repeatedly made something of a small mark.

Some politicians you look at and think, 'Has time stood still?' Annette King — shit, is she still there? How old is she now? Doesn't she have some life waiting for her somewhere . . . anywhere?

Phil Goff. Great contribution, Phil. But isn't there a university somewhere that wants to employ you?

There is actually a long list of politicians who fit into the 'been there too long' category. Some, sadly, you will never have heard

161

of, and have names you wouldn't even recognise. Not because they have had their heads down working, but because they are nonentities and entirely worthless components of parliament. To expose them now would be to give them more credit than they deserve. They are like bad wall-coverings: you pass them often, but no longer see them, if ever you did.

There is a category of politicians who burn brightly and then move on. This is the category I think I would have been in if I had succeeded in my endeavour to enter politics in 1999. Brendan Horan is one of those — no, I am shitting you. He is a complete waste of space. But Don Brash was one. Ultimately, spectacularly unsuccessful. Nonetheless, huge achievement for very brief endeavour. Sadly, like so many, he found walking away from politics too hard and had to have one last magnificent humiliation.

John Key fits into this 'burn brightly' category. As they say, 'Many a slip 'twixt cup and lip', but, given that, I don't see John waiting around for any humiliation. When his time is up, he will be one of the first to see it and disembark. Job well done!

David Shearer has the opportunity to fit into this category now. Spectacular achievement for time invested. We all now know it's not for you, David. You failed, but failed quickly. Almost everyone has said you are a decent bloke. Must be time to re-enter the frontline of life. Go — now!

God, I could go on forever. Christ knows, there are enough politicians . . .

The thing about politics I don't quite understand (and let's be frank, I understand most things very well) is the fascination we have with the most insignificant aspects of it. It is spectacular entertainment, which is lucky, as it is the most expensive entertainment most of us will ever be forced to pay for. All day and every fuck'n night we are fed a diet of minor details packaged as vitally important developments. There is no other business we scrutinise anywhere near as closely. If it weren't for politics, weather and holiday road tolls, we could reduce our news programming by 80 per cent. Only rarely does something truly momentous happen. Finding out I was paying for Shane's diet of porn was one such occasion. I feel sorry for those who have no interest in politics. They still have to pay full price for the entertainment and reap no fun from it.

You won't have picked this up from my views thus far — as I am very careful to keep my politics to myself, for fear that my well-reasoned political opinions might interfere with my impartiality — but I am a right-winger. Flirted with voting ACT on occasion, but they were such a cot-case that I only actually encouraged some family members in Epsom to vote that way for Rodney, then John. And only the constituency vote. Like some other political reporters, I don't vote for fear that doing so would infect my ability to do my job — that's shit. Of course I vote. **Only a twat wouldn't vote!**

Being impartial is living a lie. Only the completely brain-dead are truly impartial. And, with only a few exceptions, political reporters and commentators are not completely brain-dead. I want to know the views of those who report and are involved in filtering information my way. I don't want them to allow their views to interrupt or taint the information they cover in most cases, and knowing how they think helps me assess whether or not that is happening. I have given Labour as many plaudits as I have National over the years. In fact I am almost more likely to attack National as they have a greater capacity to disappoint me.

That is actually one of the disadvantages National has over Labour. Its supporters are more likely to be its greatest critics. Labour has (albeit to a lesser extent now than at any other time) a large contingent of blind supporters. For them, not voting Labour would be akin to betraying their first-born. National supporters are much more likely to be fair-weather friends. When times get tough, the smell of blood is in the air. This difference is largely due to mindset: the left are spenders of others' money; the right are creators of wealth. The left carve the pie; the right grow the pie. The left talk of caring for others; the right fund the caring. The left consider themselves worthy; the right are worthy. The left are wrong; the right are . . . right.

It is foolish to imagine that right-wingers do not care for the underclass. In my experience there is little if any difference in the world which most fair-minded people want to strive for, whether left or right. The differences are centred on how you achieve the goal. No reasonable person wants people to be uneducated, sick, homeless or dysfunctional. Both sides of politics are aiming in the same direction; they are just travelling along different routes.

THE 'WHY?' LIST:

1. Hone Harawira
2. Green's economic policy
3. Maori Electoral Roll
4. voting New Zealand First
5. co-leaders
6. MMP
7. 121 members
8. list seats
9. 5 per cent threshold

AWARDS:

- ★ Knowing when to go, going, and not coming back: Darren Hughes
- ★ Never knowing the above: Winston Peters
- ★ Capitalising on a questionable mental state: Nick Smith
- ★ Holding your lack of talent under the radar long enough to guarantee a handsome pension: Tau Henare (fierce competition)
- ★ Right time, right place, right person: Steven Joyce
- ★ I just can't help loving her: Judith Collins
- ★ I just can't help loving him: Trevor Mallard
- ★ I just can't get her out of my fuck'n mind: Metiria Turei
- ★ Who the fuck are they and why: Craig Foss (fierce competition)
- ★ If Labour want a chance of winning, I need to be leader: David Cunliffe
- ★ For the same reason, I need to be deputy: Jacinda Ardern
- ★ Biggest embarrassment on the world stage: Helen Clark (Pant-suit-gate!)
- ★ Best mispronunciation: Rodney Hyde (cacophony)
- ★ Best use of words that don't exist to construct sentences that make no sense: John Tamihere
- ★ Best-turned-out in worst fashion: Tony Ryall
- ★ Most statesman-like: Tariana Turia
- ★ Cop-out nudist: Keith Locke (body paint, my arse)
- ★ Biggest non-event: Maggie Barry (fierce competition)
- ★ Best loved by subterranean invertebrates: Peter Dunne

STOP PRESS:
AWARD FOR SUCCESS AFTER THE
MOST ATTEMPTS AT LEADING THE
LABOUR PARTY: DAVID CUNLIFFE.

- ★ Best battery-chook impersonation: Sue Kedgley
- ★ Best holder of liquor: John Banks (teetotal)
- ★ Worst holder of liquor: Photo finish (such fierce competition)
- ★ Know when to say no: Helen Clark
- ★ Entertainer of others: David Lange
- ★ Entertainer of self: Shane Jones
- ★ Best reintegration to civilian life: Alamein Kopu
- ★ Worst reintegration to civilian life: Donna Awatere Huata
- ★ Most extraordinary reintegration: Chris Carter
- ★ Most useful transexual MP: (not awarded)

OUR LEADERS IN A LINE:

BILL ROWLING (1974–1975): First PM I have a recollection of. Disaster, but nice guy.

ROBERT MULDOON (1975–1984): Great opposition leader, perhaps the best. Dangerous tyrant with drinking issue. Very impressive in very short bursts. Not such a nice guy.

DAVID LANGE (1984–1989): Intellectual. Deserved better than he got from his deputies. They were the best of times, they were the worst of times. Ultimately, a disaster.

GEOFFREY PALMER (1989–1990): Who? Did he ever want to be leader? No! Had no idea how to stand in front of a country. Disaster.

MIKE MOORE (1990–1990): Fifty-nine days of madness with the last man standing. Great after-dinner speaker. Don't expect him to wash up.

JIM BOLGER (1990–1997): Lucky buffoon with just enough mongrel to survive. Not clever enough to be truly dangerous. Not quite stupid enough to be a complete disaster. Wonderful wife!

JENNY SHIPLEY (1997–1999): She was never going to last. Capable, but out of step with the country. Everything you saw — and you saw quite a bit — was everything there was!

HELEN CLARK (1999–2008): Genius politician. Hard-working. Smarter than necessarily good for a PM. Increasingly disappointed by those around her — and, let's face it, with good reason! Arrogance got her in the end, as it often does.

JOHN KEY (2008–long may he reign!): Not interested in being a genius politician. Very capable. Works smart. Best person for the job by a country mile. Surrounded by Machiavellian wannabes and opportunists that won't get the chance to call his number!

COMMENT:

What? No Winston Peters on the list? Just shows you can only fool all of the people some of the time!

SUPPLEMENTARY LIST OF THREE:

🇦🇺 **JULIA GILLARD**: Very capable, but not at politics. Come over for coffee one day . . . soon.

🇦🇺 **KEVIN RUDD**: Cunning and politically savvy. Wouldn't trust him or want him over for coffee . . . ever.

🇦🇺 **TONY ABBOTT**: Very smart, but largely a social incompetent. Australia's newest PM. Gets credit for not falling over. God — he's here for coffee!

TONY ABBOTT'S RIGHT HAND WOMAN JULIE BISHOP IS PERHAPS THE SEXIEST MATURE LADY. I HAVE KISSED HER!

168

MONEY

Having money. Making money. Being rewarded with money. These are all good things. If you have only negative thoughts about money and associate it entirely with greed, corruption and poor outcomes, it says much more about you than it does about money, or those fortunate or clever enough to have lots of it. People who are offended by money offend me.

If you are passing your negativity on to impressionable children, you are doing them a great disservice, and potentially saddling them with your prejudice and despair. Locking them into your life of dissatisfaction and envy. You would be much better off concentrating your efforts on improving your own financial situation than criticising that of others.

A Bank of New Zealand television and multi-media campaign started in late 2012. I hoped it would be a short run, given it is hopelessly inaccurate, badly produced and yet another example of a large organisation being duped by advertising and marketing agents.

This campaign states: 'Money is neither good nor bad — it's what you do with it.' Not a particularly snappy line.

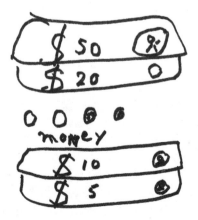

Their CMO (chief marketing officer) says that the campaign is designed to start a conversation about money. He says that New Zealanders aren't usually comfortable talking about money. Interestingly, neither are the BNZ — he wouldn't say how much the campaign had cost!

The bank needs to know this: money is *only* good. The BNZ are wrong. (And when a bank is so badly wrong about a fundamental like money, they must also be stupid! If you are a BNZ customer, alarm bells should be ringing . . . about now. P.S. Alarm bells are sometimes bad!) If money was neither good nor bad, you wouldn't need as many banks. People would not desire it as much or want to protect and grow it. Amongst other things, having lots of money gives you even more freedom. That includes the freedom to do bad things, but in no way does that make money bad.

So, if it must use a pithy line, the line the bank should be using is this: 'People are bad and good, but **money is *only* good.'**

NOTE TO THE BNZ:

I had always intended to write about money in this book, so this small chapter is not part of any conversation you have started. It is merely fortuitous that your ill-conceived campaign has given me the opportunity to highlight how bad you are with your money. You see, it is you that is bad; your money is still good. Twats.

SUPPLEMENTARY:

Small-minded people are critical of those with money. John Key is criticised by these people for being successful. They are probably right to criticise in his case. It would, after all, be much better to have someone running a country who was unsuccessful at running their own lives. Twats.

COMPOUNDING SUPPLEMENTARY:

Labour activist Conor Roberts famously compared Prime Minister John Key and rival David Shearer with the now moderately famous line: 'John Key went overseas and made 50 million dollars; David Shearer went overseas and saved 50 million lives.'

Granted, it's a snappy line. But once the snappiness wears off, the effectiveness is also gone. Without money, David Shearer would not have been overseas at all. Without the fantastically large sums of money donated to the organisation he was employed by, donated by wealthy nations, he would have saved no lives. That's none. Zero v 50 million. Not so snappy now, is it? The lives he was saving were those of the poor and dispossessed. And to do it he was using the money of the wealthy and caring.

Money is good.

PERSONAL:

I have lots and lots of money, but not as much as John Key, and perhaps — horror of horrors — not as much as David Shearer.

UPDATE:

This highlights one of the downsides of the printed word versus the electronic word. As predicted, David Shearer has called it a day. The race is on to replace him. Who will it be? How much do you care? Off to print.

STOP PRESS: RESULTS ARE IN:
3 TOO MAORI
2 TOO GAY
1 TOO BAD

OK, SO ITS DAVID CUNLIFFE.
'NO WORRIES THERE JOHN!'

SMOKERS

Where the fuck do some smokers get off?

To be fair, I have some sympathy for smokers. They are the product of our sophisticated society. A society that educated us to believe sticking a wrapped-up tube of dried foliage between your lips and setting it on fire was 'cool'.

The prime responsibility of government is to protect its citizens, and yet here they openly profit from the legal sale of consumable poison to their citizens. I know, you might say they don't profit, they merely recoup part of the cost of smoking. I don't care for your pedantacism! (Yes, that is a word in my book!) Governments would say people have become addicted, so to outlaw the production and sale of tobacco would be uncommonly cruel. Much, much crueller in fact than letting them rot from within.

I also have some sympathy for the large tobacco companies. (Who incidentally pay a great deal of tax — I do care for *my* pedantacism!) Their job is not to protect anyone. It is to make money for themselves. So in lieu of a decisive ruling from government — sell any more and you are going to jail — they must manipulate the climate to prosper. Poor darlings.

With plenty of education out there and graphic pictures of internal haemorrhaging, many choose still to smoke. Why? A desire to die prematurely, bleeding from within, or just a lack of self-control? Whatever, one of the joys of democracy is the ability to destroy yourself. A joy that socialists want to curtail by holding your hand and guiding you through their idea of your life, while simultaneously sucking the life blood out of others. Not to mention bankrupting the country in the process.

Given all that, who are these smokers who outrage me so? They are the smokers who are so offended by their own habit that they smoke at arm's length, and in doing so thrust their filthy business at me. Clearly the filth they are putting into their bodies must never come close to the plastic receptacle designed specifically for it in their cars. They tap their ash out the window in front of my car. They flick their butts out the window onto my road. Where do you get off, you filthy shit? It's your habit, not mine. On the street these awful individuals cluster and launch their toxic smog as far from their faces as they can. Presumably so their clothes don't carry the stench that will belie their disgusting pastime. Listen up, you dirty shit: you choose to smoke, own up to it. Hold your head high and fuck off!

POSSIBLE FACT:

I have been told that as you enter an operating theatre during an operation you can instantly tell if the patient is a smoker. The stench is apparently outrageous. Like an open sewer.

Though, to be fair, part of everyone's anatomy is actually a sewer, so open it at your peril.

CIGARETTE

SUPPLEMENTARY POSSIBLE FACT:

One hundred per cent of forest fires are started by smokers.

ANECDOTE:

A few weeks ago I was crawling along the I-10 in LA. My eldest daughter was by my side in the Mustang in about 30 degrees. Windows up, air conditioners on, it was almost gridlock. As I always do, I was monitoring the behaviour of my fellow citizens to be sure I didn't miss the opportunity to complain about the actions of lesser beings.

The driver's window opened on the car two up in my lane. A hand came out and the entire contents of a full ashtray was emptied onto the road before me. 'Fuck'n filthy shits!' I exclaimed, and applied pressure to the horn. No one seemed to care as I tried in vain to energise my fellow drivers to take up arms against these evil bastards, drag them from their car and set fire to them. Okay, I hadn't quite worked through a plan of retribution. In fact, I soon became the target of the apathetic. Glares, glances. 'Who is this spastic?' I could hear them thinking as they stared at me with their lifeless eyes. At that point I became aware that my daughter had adopted the stance of disassociation.

Eventually I drew alongside the offenders. A car full of trollops in their early twenties. I looked, they looked. My daughter told me to shut the fuck up. And my outrage continued . . . albeit suppressed deep inside.

OBESITY

Let's be honest. People are obese because they eat too much. There are many reasons why people eat too much. There is a grab-bag of contributing factors — lack of exercise, bad lifestyle, poor eating habits and food selection, a genetic predisposition, bad parenting, and so on. There can even be a combination of factors. But one thing is clear: if obese people did not eat as much as they do, they would not be as obese. And maybe if they were to eat much less, eat better food, and exercise, they would not be obese at all.

Our society is set up to blame itself rather than the individual for poor behaviour. For example: Bad parenting is a result of poor services. Child abuse is a result of poverty. Violence is a result of a lack of opportunity. Unemployment is a result of poor governance.

Obesity, therefore, is a result of a lack of education. It is also a result of the marketing of convenience foods, and, in general, society's fault for putting temptation in the way of people totally incapable of exercising restraint or common sense.

You know what it really is, though: some people put too much food into themselves. If that's you, stop it. Now. Sorted.

If you are a **fattie sympathiser,** you will be disgusted by this. Well, I am disgusted by you. Your constant sympathy and excuse-creation scheme are exacerbating the problem.

Fat people don't actually outrage me. What does outrage me is that, as a successful hardworking person, I have to pick up the tab for the poor decisions of others, and in many cases the care of fat-related health outcomes fits into that category. But picking up the tab for others is the subject of another chapter. And, to be

FAT

179

honest, some fat people are completely incapable of bending over, so picking anything up, particularly a tab, is way beyond them!

It outrages me when, on the very odd occasion I am forced to fly economy, like on a flight from LA to New York last year, a fat person actually occupied half of my seat. The flight attendant apologised at the end of the capacity flight when I asked for at least a partial refund as I was not given access to a full seat. Don't talk to me about the smell or the fact that liquid was seeping out of the man's arm and impregnating my clothes. It must have been low-viscosity fat!

I digress. What really outrages me, with regards to obesity, is parents who allow and even promote obesity in their children. This is nothing short of child abuse, and is a real tragedy. I have sympathy for parents trying hard, and at times in vain, to slim their children down. But for those who care not and promote and facilitate bad eating and obesity in their children, I condemn you. As you should rightly be condemned. You don't deserve to be parents, and should be punished by society, not handed sympathy.

FACT:

Some of the profit from the sale of this book goes to supplying insulin to fat people who, as a direct result of their own stupid, negligent lifestyle decisions, have contracted diabetes. Don't thank me for it, as I know you were about to. If I was able to stop the flow of money in that direction, I would. Fuck'n outrage!

SUPPLEMENTARY FACT:

I am overweight. Sometimes I make an effort to slim down, but mostly I eat too well, and am pudgy as a result. This could be directly related to my lack of education or the things that have been forced into my shopping cart by pretty labels and two-for-one specials. But I prefer to blame the government and John Key.

NOTE TO JOHN KEYS:

Stop making me and lots of the Maoris fat. We need more money so we can buy the fruits.

PARENTING

I know it's a well-worn path, but parenting really is the most important thing you can do. It is also without doubt the most rewarding. Let's be honest, there are a lot of rewarding and important things out there, and life is all about balance. But if you are going to have children, or you have them now, their childhood is your responsibility. Don't fuck it up.

Children develop a capacity to experience magic at a very early stage. It is wondrous and infectious. It should last for many, many years. For the very lucky it lasts a lifetime. It is a parent's fortunate responsibility to foster the magic, and the parent's great fortune to be able to share in the ride.

Sadly, some children are saddled with substandard parents. The very worst of these are true abusers, but they are covered in another chapter. The vast majority of parents are substandard because they are too interested in moving their own lives on to the next stage. Too concerned with themselves. Too focused on speeding their children through childhood. They have no time, perhaps as a result of working for a future, at the expense of the present.

You see, far too many parents — the overwhelming majority — don't understand one simple thing: these are the golden years. Now. Stop and experience the best of your children's childhood.

Yes, you can be absent earning money, as I was for far too much time. Yes, the money is great, and if you are successful it means you can spend it on your children. But here is the problem: by the time you have lots of it, they are not children anymore. They are always your children, but there is no going back. You can't recreate the tree-hut days when all they wanted was to stay out another hour with you. You can't tell that little girl another bedtime story, because the little girl no longer exists. She is still wondrous, and still your little girl, but changed. A bit more of the magic has gone. Squeezed out by life lessons, like 'Get in here and do your homework!' or 'Stand in that queue for registrations!' You have missed out, and they have missed out.

Good parenting is not about learning how to be a parent and following some prescribed wisdom. It is about fostering childhood and loving the shit out of the golden years. If you have one or more parenting books, throw them out now and let your children teach you how to be a parent. They are actually telling you how to do it with a signalling system you have been too busy to pick up on. If you love the shit out of them and spend the time, nothing can go wrong.

TEST:

Next time your child says 'Look!', do. Stop, crouch down, and look. Let them tell you what they see. And then, rather than tell them what it is or how it works, see it through their eyes by asking them what they think it is and how they think it works. Make it more colourful and fascinating than it already is to them. And in doing so, share some of the magic. Don't tell them what it is and move them on. That's not parenting, that's child-minding.

The best child you can produce is one who is loved and is loving. Secure and passionate about life and living. Wide of vision and bursting with enthusiasm and personality. Who gives a fuck about academic qualifications? That will come easily if the rest is in place.

If you fail to be a great parent, you are a true failure. And you should be fuck'n outraged at that. Don't blame anyone or anything else. It's down to you.

ANECDOTE:

It was a rare occasion. I was in Pak'nSave in Albany (great supermarket), shopping as quickly as possible to avoid over-exposure in the human contact department. Between 'fresh produce' and the most important area — 'wine' — I was passing through the personal hygiene aisle. I noticed a mother and son shopping for a new toothbrush. The boy, about seven years old, was dwarfed by a mind-boggling array of options. He was almost hyperventilating with the excitement of the moment.

Now here's the thing. His mother noticed. She was in the moment with him and appreciated how wondrous this was. This was the magic of childhood happening, right now. This was more important than getting home on time or doing homework or having dinner ready for the rest of the family. Frankly, this was the most important thing that was going to happen, maybe all week. And she saw it. She knew it was her responsibility to keep the magic alive. She stood back and gave him all the time in the world, and all the enthusiastic encouragement she could, as he excitedly and thoughtfully buzzed from shiny brush to brush.

After making my wine selection with similar enthusiasm, I broke with tradition and, rather than exit as fast as possible, walked via the wall of tooth care. The little seven-year-old boy was still there. He was standing with a big grin on his face, holding his selection proudly in his hand. His mother was smiling. She knew at that moment that she was the best parent in the world.

SUPPLEMENTARY ANECDOTE:

Years ago, when my children were young, I knew of a family who were at a similar stage to mine. Three young children all around 10-ish. I was working spectacularly hard and successfully to create a great future for my family. It would have been easy for me to be blind to the magic, but, as luck would have it for my children, I was a magician so all was not lost. Anyway, this other family were not doing so well in the money stakes. Shit house, etc. All they seemed to want to do was have fun with their children.

I sort of resented how comparatively unsuccessful they were, and yet how much I envied them. One day I found out that they had sold their shit house, a sort of shambolic small holding, and had bought a steel sailing ship. 'What complete fools,' I enviously thought. The father had even quit his dead-end job. What a twat. I have, naturally, completely lost contact with them and have no idea where they are now or what they are doing. However, I did hear a few years later that, by the time their children were in their early teens, they had seen the world together as a family. Apparently, I was told, they were having the time of their lives and, although surely as poor as church mice financially, they were as rich as kings in every other way. How stupid were they? Wasting their time living the golden years!

PERSONAL REGRET:

I quite often think about one moment in time. My three girls, Lucy, Sophie and Bella, were playing in a magic tree. The game was a very complicated scenario that I was never fully privy to. We had a magical house with a large, magical garden, and the magic tree stood close to the bandstand and in sight of the fairies' forest, a large deep hedgerow running the length of the front of the section.

I didn't know it at the time, but this particular moment was, I think, the epicentre of the golden years. I needed them to come into the house to get ready for some unimportant thing that I had prioritised. I remember standing and looking for far too short a time at three little girls completely immersed in a wonderland — and shutting it down.

It can never be recreated. I snuffed it out with a line like 'You can do that later.' Not now, they can't!

LEFT TO RIGHT:
LUCY – NOW 25. ONCOLOGY NURSE.
BELLA – NOW 21. MAKEUP ARTIST.
SOPHIE – NOW 23. FASHIONISTA.

PATRIOTISM

There is an interesting conundrum in New Zealand. Many New Zealanders have an over-inflated view of the significance of our country on the world stage. Simultaneously, as a country we show a huge, almost embarrassed, reluctance to take overt pride in the promotion of our country. To the point that you will often hear the country and its attempts at self-promotion criticised and put down by its own. It is also rare to find a New Zealander quick to jump to the defence of New Zealand in critical discussions. And much more likely to find one agreeing with the criticism. I have a feeling that as a country we are beginning to lose our reluctance to be overtly patriotic, but we have a long way to go.

The Australians are far advanced on **New Zealand** in the patriotic stakes. Any excuse to hoist a flag and get out the pyrotechnics is proudly embraced. As it should be.

In the United States, drugstores and supermarkets have aisles set up with patriotic merchandise. Bunting, streamers, pins and flags to adorn your home on special occasions or just every day. It's a thing! And I think it's a good thing.

Let's talk about the flag. We have a flag. It's a great flag, full of proud history, and evocative of the creation of a new land. The building of a new nation under the banner of an old but honourable world leader.

Let me be frank. We have a spectacular flag under which we can all stand proudly united. But do we? No. The Maori flag is waved in contempt — often of the New Zealand flag and New Zealand. Rather than ignoring it, our leaders and many New Zealanders buckle and concede that it may be time to change. The liberal set, already embarrassed by their own country and disloyal to it, suggest that it is time for change. In an effort to compromise, others say, 'Yes, let's adopt a new flag. Perhaps that Saatchi and Saatchi advertising hoarding? The silver fern?' After all, everything in New Zealand is either the fuck'n fern or 'all' or 'black', or both. 'Let's grow up,' they say. 'Be a nation in our own right.' Dickheads!

We *are* a nation in our own right. And rather than cower in the shadow of our history, let's be proud of it. And damn proud of the country we have built and are building. We don't need a new flag.

We need a better attitude. We don't need the Maori separatist flag flying on the Auckland Harbour Bridge or on any official structure, just as **we don't need the silver fern** fluttering like a billboard.

If you seriously think that the only thing standing in the way of uniting us as a people is a fabric symbol, you are mad. If we change our flag now, we will be changing it regularly. Do you honestly think those who want the Maori flag want the silver fern, or will settle for it? 'Oh, well, we didn't get our separatist wish, but at least we got an artist's impression of a plant on a black background! Now let's sing that great national anthem!' That's going to fly! (You won't be surprised to know that I love the national anthem.)

Back to the interesting conundrum. As a country on the world stage we are fairly insignificant; those who think otherwise are at best deluded. The world could manage without us and, worse, it knows it. But for a tiny little landmass at the arse-end of the planet, we have a great reputation with a voice that is louder than the sum total of our mouths. God, that's something to be proud of. We live in paradise, have unbelievably good lifestyles by world standards, and very good governance. We have a reputation we should all be proud of.

188

FLaG

So, as a nation that understands its place in the world, let's be feverishly patriotic and strive to promote ourselves so that we continue to thrive and grow.

ANECDOTE:

I got to SeaWorld in San Diego with my youngest daughter at opening time. We were let into the first part of the compound, but were stopped from going any further by ropes and staff until the clock struck 10. At the beginning of many lanes, there was rope, staff and 50 or so people waiting. At the ticket booths, another 300 or so people waiting in line. The clock struck 10. In unison, the staff stopped talking and smiling, and firmly planted their feet slightly apart on the ground. They held their heads high as overhead speakers played 'The Star-spangled Banner' at volume. Spectacular.

SUGGESTION:

Stand in Darling Harbour on Australia Day. Accept an Australian flag when it is offered to you for free, and wave it with enthusiasm with the 20,000 others there, waiting for the fireworks to celebrate a nation. It's not 'Say Sorry Day', it's Australia Day. And they are fuck'n proud of it!

PERSONAL:

At my residence in Auckland I have two flagpoles. The one at the entrance always flies the New Zealand flag. The larger one on the property flies not just the New Zealand flag, but flags of all nations that have particular significance on the day. At my beach house I fly mostly the Stars and Stripes. The whole large US flag set at Walgreens was just US$14 plus tax. Wrapped in a packet that exclaimed in large print: *Proudly made in the USA*. Plastic golden eagle. Metal poles. External wall-bracket connectors, screws, large flag and all. A bargain . . . Now *that's* something to celebrate.

SUPPLEMENTARY:

I have a car that I keep in America. It's a 2011 Ford Mustang. In the middle of one of the small side windows there is a sticker that I haven't removed. It says: *Proudly made by the men and women of the American Auto Industry.* I often look at other new Mustangs in the States, and I have never seen the sticker missing.

My Mustang is just a little different to the others there: on the rear window, the line *proudly born and bred* appears under a New Zealand flag.

QUEUING

With the exception of those with absolutely nothing constructive to do with their lives, or those who socialise in queues, queuing is a complete and offensive waste of life. It outrages me how often we are expected to stand patiently in line while others control our lives. Queues are a tool used by business for their convenience, not for the convenience of their customers.

Perhaps, though, for me the most agitating thing about queuing is the blind acceptance of the need for it by others. Often I will exclaim at volume 'What the hell are we waiting for?' as staff mill around, seemingly oblivious to a queue, only to be informed by fellow queuers that they are 'obviously' busy and will 'presumably' get to us as soon as they can. Don't turn on me, you fool! And what's with 'presumably'? Get more staff — or better staff. You don't deserve my custom!

When you are on your death-bed, no one will offer you the weeks upon weeks you have wasted standing in queues so that you can do important things like be with your children or just live.

It is like waiting on 0800 numbers to enquire about something or have a problem fixed, the making of which is probably the responsibility of the company that now has you on a queue on the phone in your own home. And you are not even being dealt with by a human being — it's a fuck'n android voice. This outfit you pay money to does not even think you deserve to be talked to by a living creature. Fuckers. And don't tell me that my call is important to you, you lying bastard.

Banks, Customs and Immigration arrival halls, shops, the fuck'n post office . . . Who do they think they are?

And here's another thing: why have so many check-outs? If you only intend to have three staff on, why have 25 check-outs?

Quite often you have gone to a lot of trouble to get to the store. You have done the business a great favour by calling in and selecting something. And they reward you by making you wait in line to spend your money with them. Thanks!

SUPPLEMENTARY THOUGHT:

Queuing is akin to being expected to fill in entirely useless forms. You would be surprised how often I have avoided filling out forms by simply saying, 'This is not necessary. I am not filling it in.'

ANECDOTE:

I had been standing in line for half an hour waiting to enter Disneyland with my youngest daughter, Bella. Finally, we got to the gate and were told that the ink used to write our names on the ticket was not the kind they now use. We were asked to wait, with an increasingly large group of people, for a security guard to arrive with the correct marker-pen. I said, 'No, we're going in.' The woman said we could not, as our ticket needed marking. I said to her, 'I have paid my money. I have stood in your queue. I have done my bit. You owe me an apology for holding me up. You have failed to do your bit and have let me down. This is the happiest place on fuck'n Earth, and I am due some fun!' As I walked off to find fun with Bella, the woman said, 'How will we find you?' I replied, 'I don't care.' Interestingly, (1) the world did not end for the lack of the correct marker-pen, and (2) everyone else seemed content to wait with their families for a pen to arrive!

QUESTION:

Why, when your doctor's appointment is at 2.45pm, are you still in the waiting room at 3.30pm? I thought he was professional! You trust the doctor with your health and he can't even sort out a simple client roster? If people walked out in disgust it would be sorted immediately, but instead, when the doctor says, 'Sorry for the wait', you say, 'That's fine.' No, it's not fine. It's your fuck'n life he's flushing down the toilet!

RELIGIOUS TOLERANCE

New Zealand is a Christian country. Fact. I know this partly because, when I was a little boy in Howick, Auckland, starting my stellar journey through life, I was surrounded by the God squad. On both sides of us were huge families. Five children apiece. Always attending Sunday school, church and Christ knows what else.

We were C of E, but I had little understanding of that. Mostly we were agnostic, and religious experiences were confined to boating and the beach. We were very tolerant of others' religious beliefs, though. My father would laugh himself witless at the antics of visiting Mormons, and the Jehovahs across the road provided occasional interest.

Basically, though, New Zealand is Christian. That is our heritage. It is our shared experience growing up in a Christian land. The Jehovahs and Mormons share the same experience as the rest of us growing up in a Christian land. But things are a-changing! Others are moving in in vast numbers, and they are not so happy to be part of a Christian land. They are offended by some of our beliefs and heritage. Christmas and Easter are good examples. Our progressive, politically aware leadership promotes religious tolerance as though it means we should alter our way of life in order to accommodate others. That's bullshit! Tolerance is what my dad gave to the Mormons and Jehovahs. You are welcome to hold and practise your beliefs, just don't force them on me.

When schools start adapting references to Christmas and Easter in fear of disturbing those who don't believe, it is time to shift your children to a nice Christian house of education.

If you are non-Christian and migrate to this country, suck it up or leave.

We are spectacularly tolerant, and, as a result of the large and vocal number of PC wowsers here, it is often at our expense.

God save us all!

SUPPLEMENTARY:

We are not happy to permit female genital circumcision. We are uncomfortable allowing foreigners to employ at slave rates. We require migrants to meet at least some minimum health standards in their food shops. But we seem willing to abandon much of our custom for fear we offend. What twats we are!

WRITING

I woke this morning in a very unusual state of calm. In those first few moments of consciousness I was almost completely void of outrage. Then it dawned on me: I had not finished this fuck'n book. My mind swung into the red. Fuck, I have no outrage — what I have is fuck'n writer's block. Why did I ever agree to write this bastard book? What's the point of it all? Fuck! Fuck! Fuck! (Three more words.) At this point I had been conscious for, at most, five minutes.

Now my mind was full of all the shit that people have written and had published in New Zealand. I am not just talking cookbooks, diet books, self-help books. So many words are published in this country, and, like using the internet, the skill is sifting through the chaff to find the wheat. Congratulations, you — on finding this piece of fuck'n genius.

All at once I realised the point of it all: Jesus has placed me here, at this time, to define first-rate informative communication, entertainment, and insight through writing. In this book I am truly doing God's work. And perhaps through His divine, omnipotent guidance, He walks among us through these actual words. These actual pages! Jesus fuck'n Christ, this is bigger than I first thought. This is actually the new Bible. The word of God! Shit! We're all healed.

NOTE TO RANDOM HOUSE:

Extend first print run by 10,000!

NOTE TO OTHER AUTHORS:

Really, do yourself and others the great service of calling it quits now.

PERSONAL:

I now understand the light I see . . . Let me come upon your body and into your heart!

198

TERTIARY TIME-WASTERS

Nothing betrays your total lack of sound political perspective more than vocal condemnation of the need to charge students for part of their study costs, and the need to restrict access to tertiary studies on the basis that someone is a complete fuckwit or just a lazy no-hoper. The idea that hardworking people should be forced to pay for a system that encourages 'students', for want of a better word, to study themselves into adulthood, with no responsibility to fund themselves or meet an obligation to contribute, is mindless and fraught. In other words: **the socialist dream.**

Lecturers — in many cases themselves about as useful as something with no use at all — operate in an environment often with little bearing or relevance to the real world. Subjects are defended with vagaries such as 'Anything that broadens the mind and stretches belief is beneficial.' Wankery!

We need to train the eager and capable to be the best. We need to charge them so that they have a very real understanding of the cost and of their responsibility to contribute. We need to celebrate their achievements and reward them with opportunities that they in turn maximise for our mutual benefit. And the eager and capable need to be grateful for the sacrifices others make so that they may excel.

We also need to do a great service to the lazy and stupid, and stop them from racking up a bill at our expense that they will spend decades trying to avoid repaying. If you are lazy and stupid: grow up. Get a job. Or bugger off.

If you are eager and capable, understand this: you will need to work hard all your life to prop up the lazy and stupid.

I have witnessed first-hand the unbridled wankery of tertiary study. Groups of students taking odd notes as some befuddled duffer describes the emperor's new clothes in their finest detail. As a country we just can't afford to waste money on time-consuming dross like this!

Access to tertiary study should be based on ability and enthusiasm to learn. You should not be given priority on any other basis, with the exception of those who can pay a premium to study — and in doing so create more opportunity for others to study. Being of a particular race, sex, disability or sexual preference should have no bearing on your admission. If, for example, you are a partially-sighted Maori lesbian, you should not instantly be admitted to the bush skills course you applied for.

TOP NINE COURSES TO STUDY:

1. Socialism: how to recognise and destroy.
2. Medicine: fixing the rich.
3. Science: advancements in natural selection.
4. Engineering: building with opulence for a select few.
5. Teaching: primary and secondary only.
6. Making and spending money in the twenty-first century.
7. Art: weeding out the charlatans.
8. Law: protecting the rich.
9. Trades: working for the rich.

TOP NINE COURSES TO AVOID:

1. Socialism: how to promote and foster.
2. Bush skills.
3. Feminism in eighteenth-century Japanese poetry.
4. The relevance of *Shortland Street* to the modern-day eunuch.
5. Laughter as a tool in animal husbandry.
6. Psychology.
7. Wet-nursing for the homosexual.
8. Diabetes, depicted by impressionist art pertaining to the Treaty of Waitangi.
9. Anything pertaining to the Treaty of Waitangi.

DEFINITION: TERTIARY INSTITUTION:

Large structure inhabited by socialists with over-inflated opinions of their own importance. Place to promote the growth of academic snobbery and ill-founded political beliefs. Place to rest between doing little and doing nothing, while allowing others to fund your life.

ANECDOTE:

I had an acquaintance who left school and immediately started a small panel shop with borrowed money. He risked everything for a business that consumed all his time over several years. His eagerness and unfaltering hard work saw him employ two people and pay large sums in tax. He created wealth for himself, for his employees and their families, and for the country. He told me of his fury over a conversation with one of his schoolmates, who was bemoaning a student loan of around $80,000 that he had racked up getting a qualification in something he had decided did not suit him. The panel-beater told me that it was his $80,000, and he wanted it back.

FOOTNOTE:

I asked my literary assistant how she became such a good speller, as I bellowed 'Is this how you spell "tertiary"?' She replied, 'University!' (I think she hates me!)

UNFINISHED BUSINESS

I am mostly blind to others' unfinished business. I am not of the opinion that 'if it was worth starting, it is worth finishing'. Many things are started that were not worth starting, let alone finishing. Examples would be:

- MMP — more power to idiots, more idiots to power
- the Alliance Party — what a bunch of no-hopers
- the New Zealand Party — what a bunch of opportunists
- rapid rail — like that's ever going to happen
- Hamilton — why?
- reflexology — God give me strength
- non-alcoholic beer — drinking it is just bloody ridiculous
- Concert Radio — paying for it is just bloody ridiculous

However, when it is *my* unfinished business it is a crying shame not to see it through. Unfortunately, everything I do at some stage hits the heartbeat test: I only have so many heartbeats to spare, and when I feel something is taking too many of them, my enthusiasm for whatever it is dies.

Art. I am bloody good at it, but I just lose the will to live at the thought of picking up a tool to craft a masterpiece. Writing. I have written Earth-shattering literature in my head, but the thought of— No, I just can't think of it!

At one point, I thought: children's stories. Like modern art, how hard can that be?

Let me answer that for you now: not very hard at all. Just as you always suspected. So why doesn't everyone do it? Well, for a start, too many people do. But mostly people don't, because they

203

can't be bothered. I could be bothered, but only just.

So here it is:

1. A picture of a chunk of my modern art, part one of three (two yet to be completed), currently hanging in the mansion of a celebrity!

2. The beginning and end, with no middle, of my children's story,

'Pyrmont the Noble Pigeon'.

BEGINNING: The town's crumbling cenotaph remembering the war heroes of long ago is mostly avoided by people now. It is surrounded by cracked, uneven pavement, five large trees, and some seating for old people who can't make it from the supermarket to the bus stop without collapsing into mad conversation with themselves on the poo-covered benches.

The poo is pigeon poo.

Pigeons live in this tired little area. They poo everywhere, and no one can be bothered to clean it up. Not the mad chatty old people. Not the homeless man who sometimes begs outside the supermarket near the cenotaph. (He may have his own poo problem going on. He can't even get the food out of his beard.) Not the fat man with no legs who parks his wheelchair under one of the trees for hours every day so he can watch nothing happening, when so much is going on. Not even the town's cleaners, who are almost never around. But especially not the hundreds of people who are too busy to even see the poo as they rush through this amazing place to get on with their very important lives.

MIDDLE: . . .

END: Sophie was very sad, but how wonderful was the truth.

After a long life of flying over the comings and goings of others, of being overlooked by so many, Pyrmont, the noble little pigeon knew that out of all the pigeons he alone had found his way into a little girl's heart. And in Sophie's heart he will live forever. And in her words, Pyrmont is a star. The End.

NOTE:

The above unfinished children's story should be viewed as an extraordinary opportunity. And a challenge! **I am giving it to you. No need to credit me.** It is yours, free. I will even put you onto an excellent illustrator! Just pen a 'middle' and submit it to my publishers, Random House. They are quite rightly only interested in their own financial advancement, but will reject you respectfully if it is crap. If it is not, well good for you.

Now, to the illustration. My beloved and bewildered mother, Olive, has penned a range of pigeon pictures that, for your convenience, I have assigned a letter from A–F. Just pick your favourite from those on the following pages, and the cover's done!

See. Not hard at all. The finer details can be negotiated now with your publishers, and my work is done.

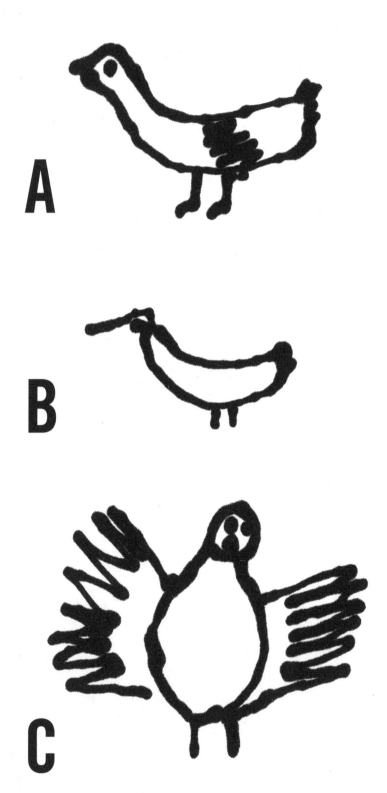

A

B

C

206

D

E

F

207

TIPPING

We live in a comparatively safe haven of no tipping, but it's creeping in. It's something we must avoid at all cost. It's insidious. And there is no going back.

In reality, what poses as tipping is often not tipping at all. It's another tax.

If you 'tip' a server, you are gifting them money for providing you with service or entertainment that exceeds their duty, and in so doing improves your experience beyond the expectation of enjoyment you could reasonably have had. You don't tip for a smile or friendly service. Why would you frequent an establishment where the staff were unpleasant? You don't tip for nice food or product. That is your expectation. All of that should be the bare fare in any business you patronise.

I frequently embarrass those around me in the States when I refuse to tip for anything other than exceptional service. (To be honest, I do quite often get exceptional service in the States!) I explain, when glared at by servers, that I can't possibly give a tip for substandard or even adequate service. Why would you? A reward for nothing? That's not how life should work.

In America, they often print guides for tourists on tipping. Hello, tax rates! They say '15–20 per cent of the bill is typical'. Typical for fuck'n what?

The fact is that Americans have accepted the gratuity as a tax, of at least 15 per cent on most things. They have accepted that companies can pay staff well under the living wage on the basis that the customer will top up their pay to a satisfactory level. Tipping, my arse. Taxing. If you can't afford to pay your staff satisfactorily, fuck off! I certainly don't want to deal with you.

It is such a treat to be served spectacularly well by someone in New Zealand who has no expectation of being rewarded further. They are just great at their job. Let's keep it that way.

SUPPLEMENTARY FACT:

Service in New Zealand is often substandard. I despise dealing with people in shops who are disinterested, ill-informed or can't speak English. It speaks volumes about the business and its owners. If they don't care enough about their customers to see them served professionally, they don't deserve to have customers. If you put up with bad, disinterested service, you are a fool yourself and part of the problem.

ANECDOTE:

I used to eat often at the Harley Davidson Café in Vegas. The ribs were — and perhaps still are — great. The fit-out is fantastic, and the servers are very good. I would often leave a tip as a result of having had such a great time. While I am the sort of person who scrutinises the bill to ensure I am never the innocent victim of fraud or error, I don't always scrutinise. So it was after the third or fifth visit to the café that I realised that they actually add a gratuity of 18 per cent to the bill before they give you the guide to tip. So in fact you are tipping in part based on the gratuity!

I'll tip your tip and raise you. Fuckers.

I have never been back.

SUPPLEMENTARY ANECDOTE:

I was once chased out of an establishment, with my US manager frantically trying to avoid confrontation, when I loudly refused to tip an appalling Hispanic man, who had barely made eye contact while serving a shit meal. I had suggested anyone who offered a tip at their shit-hole needed their heads read. Such excitement!

210

TWEETING

I am not sure why Twitter outrages me, but it does. I understand it, but I don't understand why you would bother with it. Perhaps I can see the mentally vulnerable becoming addicted for a short time, but surely no longer than a few days?

I have never tweeted, but people have posed as me and tweeted on my behalf. How do I know this? I have been told, by some of the many people who were apparently following 'fake me' on the tweet machine. The same people who had befriended another few 'fake me's on Facebook. Doesn't that expose it for the sham it is?

Why are so many people so involved in social media? Every subtle nuance of life is painfully reported in real time. Why? Yes, it is a way to communicate, but there is so much of it that it is impossible to filter. It is impossible to verify everything. Who has the time with all the pressing things to tweet? Perhaps, though, verification is unnecessary. You just want to know where Kate Hawkesby is and what she is eating.

People will sing the praises of Twitter using examples of momentous events where tweets have been the fastest way to expose the truth. These same people bore the shit out of each other with minute-by-minute accounts of eventless bus trips. Fuck, we are so sophisticated.

Next time you interrupt a social encounter in the first person by focusing on your mobile, think: What the fuck have I become? Another mindless follower of a fad that is now controlling me. Twats.

SUPPLEMENTARY:

Kate Hawkesby is in Depot eating an iceberg wedge.

FUCK OFF!

VANGUARDS FOR OUTRAGE

The vanguards for outrage are those who seek out outrage and promote it so that it might grow. They are the sort of people who create outrage by distorting something or taking it out of context and alerting people to it. They have little or no humour in them, and little or no capacity to recognise humour in others. If I gave a damn what others thought of me, these people would be the bane of my life.

If you are a vanguard for outrage, you will be having a fuck'n field day with this book. My advice to you: buy lots of copies and distribute them widely.

SUPPLEMENTARY:

If you are a vanguard for outrage posing as a journalist, you should be ashamed of yourself. My advice to you: stop misrepresenting the lives of others and get a life yourself.

THE ELDERLY

Old people are not nice just because they are old. Old people are just young people later in life. It is assumed by most that old people have a pleasant personality, but all too often, just like with people in other age groups, that is not true. In fact, automatically assuming old people are nice is quite condescending. I am not going to fall into that trap.

It seems to me that there are too many of them about — old people that is — but that may just be the circles I move in.

There should be no credit given for age when it comes to performing many tasks. Again, condescending. For instance, driving. If you can only drive safely at 30 kilometres an hour, you actually can't drive safely at all and should be in a taxi. Or on the bus. Or locked indoors, for your safety and the sanity of others.

It is criminal how Jesus rewards a hard-fought life with failing senses and, chances are, a stream of shit running down your legs. Thanks, Jesus. Something to look forward to. Thanks very fuck'n much.

PERSONAL:

When I am very old, I am going to call bad-mannered young people 'fuckers', and tell them to 'stand aside or I will touch you with my pissy hands'.

214

ANECDOTE:

Several years ago I bumped into Sir Edmund Hillary at the front door of a bank quite close to his house in Auckland. I had interviewed Ed several times, and was about to speak to him when the span of his life stopped me in my tracks. It was only a year or, so before his death, but neither of us knew that at the time. He was still a monster of a man with a craggy face like Everest itself. He was wearing sensible 'old man' clothes, which, like the man himself, belied his majesty.

I was leaving the bank just as the most recognisable New Zealander in the world was about to enter. What struck me was his obvious exhaustion as he paused midway up the four steps to the front door from the pavement; his huge hands grasping the metal handrail as though it were a lifeline slung between two mountaineers. I stopped and waited to greet him when he finally summited. We talked for a short time as he acclimatised to the thinner air at the bank's front door, and then he went in to do his business. As I descended I thought, 'These are the new Hillary Steps. Bastards to knock off for an elderly icon.'

VAGRANTS

There is no place for filthy vagrants living on our streets and under our motorways. They are antisocial and counter-productive. For the vast majority, their lifestyle is a personal choice. A lifestyle forged from dysfunction, mental illness, and bad decisions and relationships.

Let's be honest. Vagrants are dirty, smelly and often rude, threatening and offensive. Businesses pay huge sums in tax one way or another, and they deserve protection from scum pissing in their alcoves, corridors and alleyways, putting off custom and generally detracting from the business at hand. Why do we put up with these vagrants? Why don't they outrage society as much as the bastard gangs? I suppose people just feel sorry for them. Putting coins in their grubby hands so that they might perpetuate their disastrous lives.

This is New Zealand. We don't have the space issues or financial problems of many other countries. We are in the position to move vagrants on, and councils need to find a backbone and tidy up this mess. I don't care to answer any questions relating to what we might do with these smelly individuals, the options are endless. Namby-pamby do-gooders have had their chance. Just sort it — clean the streets.

SUPPLEMENTARY:

I have some sympathy for the agencies and volunteer workers who struggle to help vagrants. Give those mostly well-minded groups a break and ship these vagrants out now.

ANECDOTE:

I was leaving a supermarket in Balmain, Sydney, a city full of dirty vagrants. This one shitty mess inhabited the porch to Woolworths and essentially pissed people off with his awfulness.

As I was exiting in a line with other shoppers, there was a delay. Filthy man was confronting all the customers with his hand out and the imaginative line 'Have you got any money to spare?'

Everyone in front of me whom I could hear said, 'No, sorry.'

It came to my turn, and I said, **'Yes, I have a large sum of money to spare, but giving any to you isn't even remotely part of my agenda.'**

He wisely moved on to hunt out another victim. The interesting thing was the reaction of these middle-class shoppers with no spare cash. They applauded me with their eyes.

PHILANTHROPY

Famous people like me often either support an existing charity by being an ambassador or spokesperson (not usually by actually giving their own money away), or alternatively start their own charity. Mostly they do this to keep themselves in the public eye during down-times in exposure. I have decided that it is time to enter the fray, partly as a result of a very long down-time in exposure. And as there was no charity to meet my key concern, I am honour-bound to start one of my own.

One thousand dollars a week is all it takes to reimburse boat owners out of pocket through ludicrous expenses and depreciation. Or, worse still — those who have lost hundreds of thousands of dollars selling boats they can no longer afford or have grown tired of. Just a thousand dollars a week; that's only a few coffees a day, a nice meal out, and a facial.

Somewhere, probably at a beach property in Omaha, an out-of-pocket boat owner waits. They wait for you! They wait for you to get off your lazy arse, put your hand in your pocket and contribute to their lives. They wait for you to offer them some relief from the vexing feeling deep inside all of them: that they have been swindled out of money by their own fuck'n stupidity.

The time is now . . . Don't let a boatie spend a moment longer in remorse.

Remember: only a thousand dollars a week — that's less than sixty thousand a year. Please give generously to SWH: Skippers Without Horizons.

ACCOUNTANTS

I have had the same accountant for decades. So long, in fact, that I have gotten to know his entire family. Loveliest people. The thing with accountants, though, is that they need to be above reproach. To be good, they need to be focused and serious and . . . well, boring! Mine is quite interesting for an accountant. Loveliest people. It's just not so much Las Vegas as it is Palmerston North. Now there is nothing wrong with Palmerston North. Nothing that a fleet of bobcats couldn't fix anyway. It is safer than Vegas. More fuel-efficient. Less chance of being accosted by a purveyor of prostitutes. It's just that, all up, your Palmerston North is just so fuck'n boring.

Anyway, I have just received a letter from the company of chartered accountants that my accountant works alongside. They have very exciting news, they are pleased to announce. I know, I can almost feel the collective blood draining from our veins. So the thing is this: they are merging with another group, of— No, not acrobats. Not deep-sea divers. No, not caribou hunters or sled drivers. Now any of those could possibly justify the 'exciting news' claim. In fact, it is *bad* news in the excitement stakes, I'm afraid. They are, it seems, merging with another group of accountants.

Just before we slip into a coma, there is something else. It seems I have been invited to a 'function', which, if I accept, will give me a unique opportunity to 'meet the team'. Light refreshments will be served. (Probably nothing too hot, or tricky to hold, or foreign.) As there is no mention of the on-site availability of a defibrillator, I have decided to stay away. The excitement caused by me slipping into unconsciousness would be too much.

228 ALMOST THE END.

ALCOHOLISM

Hello. My name is Paul, and I am an alcoholic. I know this because my father, late in his life, announced that he was an alcoholic, and when I looked slightly surprised he gave me his definition of alcoholism, and said he clearly met the criteria. My father's definition is 'someone who needs a drink'. It doesn't relate to the amount you drink. (He drank roughly a bottle of wine a night.) It is the need to drink. If ever you think, 'Shit, I need a drink', then you, in my father's book, are an alcoholic.

So, as my father's son I follow his definition and know myself to be an alcoholic.

There are other definitions, and, if you spend most of your life blind drunk and attend meetings with other slightly remorseful soaks the rest of the time, you might be offended by my statement. Well, take it up with my father — even dead he will give you a run for your money.

For me, it is a wonderful distraction from day-to-day life. And I am constantly looking for wonderful distractions for fear I might actually get something done.

I sit in the conversation area in my formal lounge and look over the rim of a wonderful glass of red wine. I stand in my garden, surveying all I have crafted in Nature, and sip a magnificent red. Or a shit one. The difference can be paper-thin. I just experience the moment with, at times, quite a cheap little number. It makes my magnificent moments a bit more . . . magnificent. What can be wrong with that?

Wine

222

In fact, I love my alcoholism. It makes me a better man. It somewhat bothers some of those who love me, but that is only because they think it may overwhelm me one day. Well, it almost definitely won't! On the comparatively odd occasion I pour a glass before 10am, it is only to finish a bothersome bottle that has found itself prematurely abandoned from the night before. I take the glass to the spa and remind myself how lucky everyone is that I am alive.

NOTE:

Although I have touched on this many times in this book, I feel it appropriate to reiterate here my complete disregard for the personal judgement of others. It is extraordinarily liberating to not actually give a shit. There will be those who criticise this book for God knows what. Actually, I can think of one or two things myself. Well, good for them. Their criticism says much about them, little about me. And if I am exposed as less than perfect, the liberator of that information has missed the whole point, as many will. It's just me. And I pretty much don't care. Try it if you can: I recommend it.

ATTRACTIVE PRICING

Am I the only person who still gets disappointed when I see the words 'Up to' or 'on some stock'? It's a problem created largely by font size. You approach a shop, attracted by a promise of '70% off sale', only to find it is *almost* a whole sentence, but includes

words in tiny type. 'Up to **70% off sale** on some stock.' Bastards.

'Oh, that's nice. How much is that?' 'Well, sir, that is new stock, so it is not included in the sale.' 'I see. So the good stuff that people might actually want is full price?' Bastards.

Then there are the racks that say 'All stock from $25'. What's the point of that? You could have a sign on a car yard that said that. Nothing actually has to be $25, it just has to be above $25 on that rack. Oh, surprise — it is!

This kind of misrepresentation is sometimes so contradictory that you have to challenge it.

In Sydney, I took my youngest daughter, Bella, into a clothes shop emblazoned with signage that said 'Everything in store $10 or less'. We went in with her last few holiday dollars, and she selected three items and presented them at the counter. One item was $10, one $12 and one $16. What the fuck? Impossible! From the outside, you were unable to see into the store for multiple signs boasting 'Everything in store $10 or less'.

'How can this be?' I inquired. Look closely at some of the signs: 'Some stock excluded!' Sure enough. In small print on one of the many signs, the words 'some stock excluded'. I pointed out that

'everything' is not an ambiguous word. You can't

exclude any stock, because there is no stock left to exclude as *everything* in store is $10 or less. Bella left two items behind. I flirted with the idea of a career in law. How could we live with ourselves supporting a lie? Illiterate bastards.

THE 99-CENT RUSE:

Can there be anyone left on Earth who is attracted to a price on the basis that it is well under the next dollar, due to the use of 99-cent pricing? So many businesses still use this old technique that dates back to the caveman. Mammoth steaks — $3.99 per kg. Sorry, 'per lb'. Obviously cavemen were pre-metric. However, they did have access to the odd cent or two. No, pre-metric — they were pennies. Fuck!

Nowadays things are rounded, so, unless you are purchasing a lot of items at once, you are fucked.

I go to an Indian takeaway where everything ends in '99'. Sample menu: Butter Chicken $13.99; Lamb Rogan Josh $13.99; Lamb Saag $13.99; Chicken Tikka $13.99; Plain Naan $3.99 . . . They round up everything, always — even when you pay by card — thus rendering the whole thing completely pointless. But, I have asked myself, would I still go there if the curries were $14 each? Probably not.

ANECDOTE:

BevMo! is a liquor outfit in the States. And I love liquor! They always have sales for ClubBev! members. I am one of those. On my last trip to a BevMo! I couldn't believe my eyes. A five-cent wine sale. Can it be? A bottle of wine for five cents? Well, almost. It was only some wines, and you had to purchase a full-priced bottle to go with every five-cent bottle. But a full-priced bottle at BevMo! is only about $4.50, so that means two bottles of wine for $4.55 plus tax. God bless America.

DISCLAIMER:

H istorical currency references and prices relating to cavemen may be inaccurate at time of publishing.

BENEFICIARIES

One word for you: gratitude.

Countries are judged on how well they look after their most needy, and from where I stand New Zealand can be very proud. The only glaringly obvious problem with our social welfare policy, though, is that as a country we are a soft touch for those wanting a free ride. Many of them antisocial and counter-productive. Breeding zones for dysfunction and dissatisfaction.

Every New Zealander has a responsibility to be a good citizen

and contribute. For some, it is hard to contribute and, through no fault of their own, they need the support of the greater community. That is perfectly acceptable, and in return for that support there should be a gratitude that the greater community is pulling together to prop up the individual. The beneficiary can be expected to meet certain criteria that must include being a good citizen — living responsibly and in accord with the best goals of our society. Beneficiaries should come under greater scrutiny than others as they live by the grace of others.

Why should any taxpayer be forced to facilitate the lives of those who take no responsibility for themselves and who care not for the hand that feeds them? Why should the children of hardworking parents go without because society is forced to support an increasing number of dysfunctional arseholes? Why should those who genuinely need support be cut short at times because too many bludgers are standing in front of them in the queue?

We need to be aware of the critical balance between those

who support and those who are supported. You cannot grow the prosperity of a country and its people when too few are supporting too many. The current government is making steps in the right direction to toughen up on beneficiaries, but it always amuses me how many challenge the idea that any beneficiary should be expected to take responsibility for their own life. It belittles the goals of beneficiary advocates when they blindly suggest that these people are in some way special and untouchable.

So, what do you do? As a country we don't accept drink-driving. We used to, but no longer. We have little tolerance for violent offenders, although there are still those who offer all the excuses for offenders they can. We need to ignore the apologists and grow a collective backbone when it comes to benefit abuse. It is not about a lack of compassion — it is about targeting those who need our compassion, and forcing scumbags and bludgers to step up. You do this by taking control of their lives and reducing their options. Bludgers should not be able to afford cars or luxuries of any kind. They are at best second-rate citizens, and should be treated as such. If your contribution is to live the life of a bludger off the back of hardworking citizens, your life should be miserable by comparison to the hard workers.

NOTE TO BENEFICIARY BLUDGERS:

You pay no tax. You contribute nothing but problems. You are stealing from genuinely needy beneficiaries, and from society in general. And don't tell me you pay tax out of your benefit — that's bollocks. You can't pay tax with money you take from the taxpayer.

You know who you are. (Can you even read?) Get a job. Be a good parent. Show gratitude and be a positive contributor. I wish your free ride was coming to an end!

NOTE TO THE GENUINELY NEEDY:

By supporting the faux rights of bludgers you do yourselves a great disservice.

NOTE TO SOCIALISTS AND THOSE WHO BELIEVE COMPASSION COMES FROM THE BLIND SUPPORT OF ANYONE WHO WANTS IT:

Your low-rent attitude devalues our country. Let's be aspirational. Cradle-to-grave is out-of-date, unaffordable and undesirable.

NOTE TO THE CHILDREN OF BLUDGERS:

There is a better life. Your options in life are truly exciting — take them. You have been set a very bad example, but surmount it and excel. Break the cycle! Don't expect me to make excuses for you, and don't make excuses for yourself.

CHILD ABUSE

It is perhaps **the very worst crime it is possible to commit:** child abuse.

Why would you ever bother trying to rehabilitate those responsible for the worst forms of child abuse? These animals and their apologists should be put to death. There should be no second chances. Children need love, care and energy, and if they are shown none of these, ship the children out. Then neuter the evil bastards that neglected their duty of care.

New Zealand has an abysmal record of abusive child-rearing, and one of the reasons for it is the bevy of apologists lining up to offer what they consider to be mitigating reasons for the abuse. That in itself is a form of child abuse. As a country we need to walk the talk on child abuse. No second chances. No mitigating factors. If you are guilty of this crime, you are done.

Some of the best parents had poor upbringings themselves. Some of the best parents can be found struggling with life in underprivileged households. Households they fill with love. These people still know the wonder of the opportunity to foster life. Their efforts are devalued when our society goes soft on abusers.

NOTE TO GOVERNMENT:

So many services. So many departments. So many taxpayers' dollars spent by so many experts. So many fuck'n reports. And so many damaged and dead children. Don't allow democracy to stand in the way of stopping the carnage.

231

CHILDBIRTH

You will hear people say it is a miracle, or use such phrases as 'the miracle of birth'. This is not of course meant literally. If it were a true miracle it would probably not be happening hundreds of billions of times everywhere on Earth every second. Bugs, birds, fish and, yes, ladies. Reproduction is as close to the opposite of a miracle as you can get. In humans, particularly, it is not even clever. It is so easy that it happens thousands and thousands of times a year by mistake. Those who are the best at it are often among the most stupid examples of the race.

Some people who find it hard to reproduce and angst over it for years, spending many thousands of dollars on treatment only to fall pregnant naturally, will often describe the resulting life as a miracle child. This is completely false. The fact is that Nature sometimes fucks up and sometimes comes good. Nature just does its thing. We might angst, and we might tinker, but Nature just does its thing.

It has nothing to do with a God either. It is not a blessing. It is not a curse. It is Nature. If God were able to bestow a child on a childless couple living a lovely life with enough money to tinker with the reproduction business, don't you think He would throw a bone to the thousands of children born to poverty and war only to live a short and tortured life before dying? Wouldn't He prevent the conception?

MIRACLES:

I am reminded of a deep discussion I had with Peter Williams QC. We were on a yacht, becalmed mid-ocean. The night sky was full of stars. 'Life on Earth is a miracle,' he said. 'The odds against everything necessary for life on our planet happening so that we might look up at this sky, with this infinite number of stars and planets and galaxies, are so great it proves the hand of God at work.'

I was of the opinion it proved the exact opposite. With infinite possibilities it was entirely impossible this series of unlikely events would not have happened somewhere. It was also highly likely that the inhabitants of the outcome of it happening would use the word 'miracle' to describe something entirely natural.

233—

SERVICE STATIONS

You know what I want from a service station? Fuel. That's it. On the rare occasion I need something else, let me find it myself or ask for assistance. Don't offer me fuck'n chocolates or shit from wicker baskets on the counter. Don't sell me on the latest promotion or competition as you thrust some scratchy into my hand or slide some explanatory note across the counter. Do me a favour and cut half a cent from the price of a litre of fuel and do away with the bloody supermarket-café shit. Oh, and I'm not collecting miniature dinky cars either!

Also, it is one thing to take the service out of service stations and expect me to do all the forecourt work myself (I actually prefer to do it myself), but why do I have to queue at your counter to pay? And make sure you fill the water cans. Make sure you have window cleaners with bristles and sponge centre intact. While you are at it, perhaps a squirt of suds in the black water that barely covers the bottom of the broken bucket would be nice. Say, once or twice a year you could wash down the forecourt, too.

As for paying before you pump — that's the final straw, you Nazis! So you want me to park, walk inside and stand in your queue to leave a credit card. Go back and fill my car, and then return to stand in another queue to settle. And buy your fuck'n chocolates. Give me a mop and I'll clean your filthy lino while I'm at it! Christ, we have come a long way in customer care. I know there are shits who will rob you blind, but do some profiling. Look at me and my car. Do I seriously look like I am going to do a runner? There must be a more convenient way to protect your business that doesn't require the extreme inconvenience you force your customers to put up with.

The fact is: life is far too short to be fucked around buying petrol.

ANECDOTE:

It was one of those rare occasions when I wanted something other than fuel. I wanted a car wash. Now, I dislike automated car washes, as I am of the opinion that they are either hopeless or, alternatively, will scour the shit out of your car. I was driving a rental, though, and as everyone knows rentals are completely bulletproof. They will not be scoured, can't be dented or scratched, and never need water or oil. I waited in line to purchase a chit with a code to enter into the car-wash machine. Another stellar customer-oriented experience.

When I got to the counter, I said, 'I would like to purchase a car wash.'

'Car wash isn't working. Do you want chocolate?' The bastard, putting me to all that inconvenience and now expecting me to buy his expensive fuck'n chocolates.

I replied, 'Yes. Are they free?'

'What do you mean?' this moronic bloke said.

'Oh, I thought you were giving away chocolates to all the people you inconvenience,' I said — and just left. The concept of customer care was blowing his mind.

NOTE TO BP:

am not entirely sure why I hate you a little more than the other bastard oil companies, but I do.

NOTE TO THOSE WHO CONSTANTLY COMPLAIN ABOUT FUEL PRICES:

Have you ever wondered why you are prepared to pay double the cost of a litre of petrol for a litre of bottled water in a dairy? It is so much easier and cheaper to produce and bring water to market. You fools.

236

TAX

It's a fuck'n outrage how much tax I pay. This is personal. I qualify for fuck-all and take advantage of even less. I have contributed not only personally, but also by creating extra taxpayers at huge personal expense, who like me are net contributors. How much tax is it fair to expect one person to pay? Why should you have to pay more tax just because you earn more, because you are smarter or work harder? Seriously, pause and answer that question. Why is it right that Paul Henry pays so much fuck'n tax?

Obviously there are people who need assistance, and a small number of community items that must be purchased. Oh, and a fuck'n government we have to keep in Jack Daniels. But why am I being sucked dry? How am I expected to fill the tank on my boat? There are no fuck'n vouchers at WINZ to help with that!

Back to my earlier question. Did you answer it, or did you just say, 'Because you can fuck'n well afford it, Mr fuck'n Henry!' Well, I don't want to have to pay it. I want to buy another car, and in doing so pay more GST. Now GST is a fairer tax. The well-off pay much more in GST because they spend more. Yes, they *do* spend more! But it is my choice to spend more. I might pay tens of thousands in GST on one car purchase versus the chance to pay less than five thousand in GST on a modest new car, that to be honest will almost certainly run better.

The well-off have much more expensive lives. Houses, cars, travel, exotic pets, spoilt children, costly lovers, stupid fuck'n boats . . . It all takes its toll and it all has to be maintained. It also keeps the wheels of commerce rolling. Employing people and consuming products. And you can't do as much of it if you are paying too much tax.

237

There are better ways, it's just that for some reason they don't seem to work in real life. On paper they are perfect. They rely on 'trickle-down'. That is where, say, for example that lovely Owen Glenn finds he is paying 50 per cent less in tax and immediately celebrates by giving more money away and shouting himself another super-yacht. Isn't it so much better that Owen gets another super-yacht with his money, than a bunch of MPs spend his money on a luxury fact-finding mission to Kazakhstan?

We need to encourage the smart and hardworking to be smarter and work harder. We need to have great incentives to acknowledge the risks that those who invest in speculative ventures make. A great way to do that is to allow them to keep more of their money. That way, trickle-down will kick in. If only it worked.

I am a fan of a flat rate of tax. First ten thousand in personal income, tax-free; everything else, 25 per cent for everyone. It is fair, apart from the fact that high-earners still pay more by sheer volume of income — but the thankless hordes will like that. Well, not actually like it. They won't be happy until the rich and hardworking are poor and lazy like them. Shit, who will pay then? That's the flaw in the tax system we have now!

ALTERNATIVE TAX SYSTEM:

On the average wage in New Zealand over a full working life, you will struggle to pay $1 million in income tax. You will naturally also be paying supplementary taxes in GST, petrol, your rates and so on. High-earners who pay the lion's share of tax in any country will pay well in excess of $1 million in income tax, so why not cap income tax at, say, $2 million in a lifetime for any one individual? Once an individual has paid $2 million in personal income tax, that's it. No more. You would need to be vigilant to make sure other income is not syphoned through qualifying individuals, but all that is possible. How many would come here to live tax-free? You have done your bit — thanks, and welcome. If you wanted to go tax-free immediately, just write a top-up cheque to the government and you are free.

ANECDOTE:

I once got close to losing my licence through multiple speeding infringements. Just before my points topped out, I received a letter from the police or Land Transport or some other outfit. It had a picture of a grieving mother on one side, and on the other a letter ostensibly from her to me, advising of the risk I posed to the mothers of other children who have yet to be killed by speeding drivers such as me . . . Not a bad idea. Well, why don't I get letters from those who benefit from the outrageous amount of tax I pay? A picture of a beneficiary on one side, and text itemising how grateful they are that I contribute so much to their lives. Perhaps I could receive these from staff of government departments, or politicians?

Dear Paul,

Just a note to thank you for your continued forced support.
Last week I watched two porn movies, drank five litres of vodka, and travelled to France on the back of . . . well, you.
Here is a picture of me dining in a lovely bistro just a short limo-drive from the Louvre.

Yours sincerely,

[insert name of MP]

239

QUESTION:

If you can get a chit from WINZ for a TV and DVD player, isn't it only fair that prostitutes are tax-deductible? (For all I know, you can get prostitute chits from WINZ!)

LOCAL GOVERNMENT:

Why does it cost so much to run? Fuck, they are forever empire-building. It's water, roads and sewerage. Mow a few lawns, keep a few parks, and hold a few trinkets in a museum. That's it. If I don't need a civic reception in a 'Cloud', Len, no one does! We are well on our way to having the most perfect city we can't afford to live in. Why don't all the empire-builders go rail and rapidly fuck off?

It is not just Len's Auckland. There are Lens all over New Zealand. Some better, not many worse!

IT'S LIKE YOU'RE IN MY HEAD, MR HENRY

Dear Mr Henry,

I just can't believe the things I am reading in your book. I always thought we had similar beliefs, and so often I agreed with what you said on the telly, but in this book it's like you're in my head.

Like you, I also distrust socialists. Fuck it, I hate them.

I am just the same as you with the homos, too. Let them do what they want, so long as they do it quietly and out of the sight of the wee ones, I say.

I can't stand the fuck'n lazy bastards who spend my money on movies, lotto and glue. If it weren't for them I could afford to spend more time on my boat with my friends Chrystal, Lacey and Tallulah.

And as for the fuck'n bastards who come here and take our jobs. Fuck'n foreigners. Lazy bastards.

What do you think of all the unwanted pregnancies? Fuck'n slutty youth these days. Little rutters, I say.

And as for the towel-heads — Paul, you've given me strength.

Anyway, more power to you, Mr Henry. I am going to pass your book on to some of my mates. I think one or two of them might be Labour voters. Slit my fuck'n wrists.

This book should be compulsory reading at the universities. Full of dopey greenies and lefty dickheads.

Good for you, I say. Thanks for saying what everyone should agree with.

Yours,

Norman Smythe
Motueka

P.S. Any thoughts on bestiality?

Dear Mr Henry,

It's like you're in my head! I am embarrassed to tell you that I was a Labour-voting solo mother on the benefit, so it is a miracle I even had the good fortune to come across your amazing, life-changing book. But I did, and you have awoken something in me. Since reading your book, cover to cover, I have gotten both a job and an abortion, and I plan to withdraw from my part-time university course 'Maori for beginners'. Thank you for turning me into a valuable, contributing member of society. I hope I can make up to you all your taxpayer dollars that I have wasted. Please accept, as a token, the enclosed marine petrol vouchers.

Yours with thanks,

Beverly Shamlan
Rotorua

243

2kk

Dear Mr Henry,

I just wanted to let you know your book has transformed my life. Well, actually it has transformed the way I think about my life. It's like you're in my head. It's like I am reading a book I have written. Although I would never write it, and I will never speak out loud my support for it. Whenever I mention your name to my friends and acquaintances, and to colleagues at the secondary school where I work, I am always told you are a complete cretin. So I stay quiet. I just want you to know you are not alone.

Sincerely,

Anonymous

245

THE ORIGIN OF . . .

LESBIANISM:

Although there had been some genetic abnormalities and abominations of social norms in the female race prior to the 1980s, which saw females gravitate to other females for comfort and sexual pleasure, the numbers were very small. These freaks were simply known as bewildered deviants, shunned by society and made to live their lives of mischief in shame and solitude. Mostly they ran bike shops or worked as travelling minstrels. Lesbianism proper was not invented until the early 1980s. It was seen as an entertaining distraction for weary men, and so was promoted as a way to launch the internet by Al Gore in the United States of America. It has subsequently become almost as popular as the internet itself, with some religions now recognising it informally as a legitimate alternative lifestyle for the less-attractive woman. Men have lost none of their initial attraction to it as a form of entertainment, and lesbian internet sites remain the most popular sites to this day.

AFFAIRS:

It is how I met both of my current lady friends, and how you probably met yours. Affairs initiated by men have been with us since the great Dust Bowl of the early to mid-1930s, centred in the Oklahoma Pan Handle. They started completely by accident and entirely innocently. Men, confused by depression, overwork and poor nourishment, were unable to distinguish their women when covered in dust, from the lady folk of other men. The resulting sexual excitement was so appealing that the rest is history. And just like the Dust Bowl itself, when the dust finally cleared, the true devastation was apparent and very hard to reconcile.

Women do not initiate affairs because they have no sex drive to speak of, and because their senses are more highly tuned than male senses, meaning they can more easily detect the differences in items covered in dust. The intrinsic desire to clean things also stems from this event in history, and is the origin of the common phrase: 'On your hands and knees, woman — the place is a mess and my pants have fallen down.'

THE NEW ZEALAND LABOUR PARTY:

In 1852, the famous explorer and adventurer David Livingstone was trekking along the mighty Zambezi when he came upon a small tribe of criminals. Initially terrified, he soon realised they were relatively harmless due to two things. First, their numbers were small, and, secondly, they all held the same socialist beliefs that were so unworkable that Livingstone presumed the group was doomed to a dismal and eventless life of misery. Attracted as he was to anthropological science, he decided to relocate these simple, bewildered individuals to a new land discovered only a hundred years earlier by a relative of his, Captain James Cook. Once liberated in the ripe country of New Zealand, this small tribe ran amok and thrived in a way no one could have imagined. They formally launched their ill-conceived plan for life as a political movement in 1916 and called it 'the New Zealand Labour Party'. To this day it attracts pick-pockets and the politically bewildered, and increasingly struggles to be seen as relevant. It has evolved little since being extracted from the African jungle.

VERY RICH PEOPLE:

The first very rich person was Jesus Christ. His father, Mr Christ Snr (known as 'God') commissioned a man called Noah to build him the first super-yacht. **This story has been bastardised** through history, largely due to Mr Christ's inclusion of a zoo on board. This then became a dalliance of the rich, to capture and house large collections of exotic animals. While none has come close to the legendary menagerie of Mr Christ Snr, a Mr W Hearst and a Mr M Jackson, both of the United States, were among the many rich individuals to run personal zoos as an amusement.

Many distrust the filthy rich. This is damned unfortunate, as some of them hold the key to others emulating their wealth. Do not fear or distrust the filthy rich. Copy their work ethic and risk your own money in the hope that you may one day be among them. Incidentally, the term 'filthy rich' is not as derogatory as it sounds. It refers to the fact that, as individuals, many of them were indeed filthy. Some still are. You could track them down by following the shit trail they leave in their wake. They never have to consider cleaning up after themselves, or for that matter at all. Staff were, and are, there for that.

Remember: The rich run the world because they are the risk-takers and investors that the world relies on to operate. The miserable poor rely on the rich for sustenance, although they show them little gratitude at times.

248.

Noah's Ark

249

FURTHER BUSINESS

CARS:

It is hard for me to reconcile the amount of money I have lost in my desire to have a clutch of wonderful driving machines. I have haggled tirelessly to purchase a car, all the time knowing it was probably going to be a disaster to own. On two occasions I have convinced myself, despite devastating proof to the contrary, either that an elderly Rolls-Royce is not a licence to financial despair, or that the one I am currently in love with is the exception to the rule. Neither of them was! I find myself condemning those who purchase diabolically boring vehicles, and those awful hybrids that just pretend to be cars.

Why have I polluted my life with a love of cars? Why, at my very old age, am I looking to buy an extra, very expensive sports car that I know will cost a fortune to run? It is not just that I hate greenies and I know that it flies in the face of all they hold dear. I think it is mostly that I just can't grow up. If only I could stop myself buying this next car . . . think how much more money I would have to spend on my boat!

MORE FURTHER BUSINESS

BUREAUCRACY:

Forms for the sake of forms. Questions for the sake of questions. It sucks the life blood out of you and doesn't give a shit about the value of your time. Bureaucrats should be put in their place. They are servants of the public — read them the Riot Act. Now where did I file away the Riot Act?

DOG OWNERS:

You have to remember at all times that it is you who loves dogs, not me. Keep the fuck'n thing to yourself. I don't want to see it or see any indication that it exists. I don't want to hear it or smell it, and I certainly don't want to be smelt up by it.

PEOPLE WHO JUST STOP:

What kind of moron are you? You are in a flow of pedestrians and you stop walking. You meander mindlessly into a stream of people at the mall and stop. At the top of the escalator, you stop. You are an arrogant fuckwit! I just want to stab you in the heart. Oh, your child needs checking — you just stop and lean over the pram and fiddle with the bloody infant.

252

We are all waiting for you to sort your fuck'n self out so that we can get on with our lives. Who do you think you are? You dirty fuck'n stopper!

KIM DOTCOM:

Sorry, but where did this love affair we seem to have with Kim Dotcom come from? Why do people gravitate towards him? Is it that he is so big that he has his own atmosphere to which people are drawn into orbit? Why is his word considered worthy of reporting *ad nauseam*? Why is his account of events given any more credit than the accounts of others? What a peculiar bunch the feral brigade is!

253

FURTHER, FURTHER BUSINESS

EXTENDED WARRANTIES:

Just fuck'n ridiculous. You have spent $300 on a phone, and they have talked you into a $49 extended warranty. It is going to give you two further years of peace of mind! Really? I don't think so. First, the Consumer Guarantees Act gives you that for free, and, secondly, did you ask about the exclusions? You will probably drop the bloody thing before you leave the store — warranty void. As soon as you get home, it will slip out of your clumsy hands into the sink — warranty void. On top of that, you will be well fed-up with the damn phone in a year, if you are lucky enough to still have it then, and will be desperate to get rid of it. In short: do not buy an extended warranty. If you must, just hand an extra $49 to the retailer for shits and giggles. It will be just as useful to you.

ROLF HARRIS:

It is an outrage how softly the media treated the Rolf Harris sex scandal story when it was breaking. Especially the English and Australian media. It wasn't about pre-judging, it was about reporting the facts of the matter, and the media sat on newsworthy information for months and months. Why? Only the media knew — they were outside his home in England as he was

254

being questioned by police. They basically kept it to themselves. Harris was described as 'an elderly male entertainer', when the use of his name was entirely appropriate, in fact essential! Was he seen as untouchable because his questionable hands had touched the Queen? Was it because he was a very old icon with a backdrop that formed the framework of our lives? Almost anyone else and the media would have had a field day. Just shows that we have not come that far since the great Jimmy Savile cover-up.

MANNERS:

If you want to sound dated and irrelevant, you bemoan the lack of manners in society. Seriously, though. Why are people so fuck'n rude and selfish and just shitty? Children — what's with their attitude? They are often horrible to old people. Don't they realise old people probably have bits of shit sliding down their legs? They should show some understanding. What's with smart-fuck'n-phones sucking the heartbeats out of personal encounters? Can't people see the folly in their ways? Fuck, who says 'folly'? Maybe I have become dated and irrelevant . . .

LIBRARIES:

New Zealand needs only three libraries for books: one very big library and two smaller ones, renamed 'book museums'. Books are (and this is odd coming from someone writing books and wanting to sell them) old-fashioned and losing relevance as a form of communication and entertainment. But, most importantly, as a reference tool a traditional library is hopeless compared to the library in every home. The internet — all of the books and other stuff are there. So we only need a few rooms with computers for the poor, not libraries. If you want to drop your children off to be entertained by some volunteer clown so you can top up your Botox in peace, there are umpteen other places to do it. Close down libraries and save ratepayers' money.

FINAL FURTHER BUSINESS

RUGBY AND OTHER SPORT:

What is wrong with me? By my own admission I am almost two-thirds male, and yet I have an almost total disregard for sport! I see it as a healthy distraction for others. On so many occasions I have managed to bluff my way through conversations on the subject of rugby or quoits only to give up and say, 'Fuck, can we just talk about something else?' I once shared a domestic flight with Richie McCaw — nicest guy. He knew, and threw me a bone. We talked about gardening and furniture, but I sort of promised I wouldn't talk about it! Fuck, just imagine if that plane had gone down? You would have had to turn the lights out on New Zealand: no Paul, no Richie . . . no point.

NOTE TO AIR NEW ZEALAND: The President and Vice President of New Zealand should never fly together.

CALL CENTRES:

Know this: your call is not important to anyone. There is no such thing as a priority queue, and, if there were, you wouldn't be in it. Your opinions are not valuable, and, if they were, you wouldn't be waiting in a system monitored by an automated voice. Businesses that don't give a shit for the value of your time will squander it mercilessly. Treat them accordingly.

257

COLD-CALLING:

An invasion of your privacy. It's dinner time, and you have so many better things to do than run to the phone and try to bat away a fuck'n cold-caller, who is working for someone who doesn't give a shit about you or how important your private life is. It's the job from hell for the caller, but you owe it to yourself not to say things like 'Thanks for the call' or 'Call back later', or ever use the word 'sorry'. Don't waste your precious time. Stop them in their tracks with a pleasant 'Never call again. Goodbye!'

PRONUNCIATION:

Before you worry about getting the Maori language right, concentrate on your pronunciation of English. Start with the correct pronunciation of the word 'pronunciation'. Look at the spelling — there's the clue!

Here's another: it is 'kilometre', as in 'centimetre' or 'millimetre'. I know it is not the end of the world, but it fucks me off a bit!

POLITICAL ZEALOTS OF ALL PERSUASION:

No one person or group is always right. (I am the exception that proves that rule.) Blind support is just that, and comes from ignorance.

FAUX COMPASSION:

You should almost never show compassion if you don't feel compassion. It is almost always shameful.

SHIT THAT DOESN'T DO WHAT IT PURPORTS TO DO:

There is money to be made from it. Two phrases spring to mind: 'buyer beware' and 'a fool and their money . . .' If you have been genuinely duped, take it back and cause a hullabaloo.

259

PARKING FEES:

Perhaps the biggest rip-off we have to live with. Don't complain about the cost of petrol or milk until the fuck'n councils stop ripping us off for parking in our cities! *Our* cities, not theirs. Local body politicians who are too incompetent to make it in the real world see parking as a cash-cow, when in fact it is the key to revitalising city centres. Rapid rail, my fuck'n arse.

FAUX MYSTIQUE:

They are just doctors, lawyers, professors, surgeons, judges, bank managers, politicians. They just hold down jobs like you probably do, and are due no more respect than you or anyone else. With the possible exception of lecturers, consultants and life coaches. They deserve slightly less respect.

CLIMATE DOOMS-DAYERS:

Look you fuck'n idiots: we're still here. Oh, it's a nice day. Oh, I didn't need my flippers to go to the shops after all . . .
Zodiac for sale!

GREENPEACE AND OTHER PIOUS INTERFERERS:

See above.

ANTI-WHALING BRIGADE:

One day, when we can all walk to Rarotonga on the backs of a distressed over-populated whale pod, stuffed in a once-vibrant Pacific, you will know it was **just for scientific research.** You can say sorry then.

261

TAXIS:

Does anyone know where we are? Can anyone speak English? And fuck, can you smell that?

WINE SERVED TOO COLD:

What aspect of the word 'chilled' do some purveyors of wine not understand? One of the best ways to render a wine flavourless is to freeze it, you fuck'n dickheads!

LYING:

Essential part of life. Without it we are fucked. Example: I am fully supportive of that investment in the wheelchair ramp. Or: That was fantastic — I am a big fan of interpretive dance.

GRANDEUR:

Why can't people see how nice things could look if a bit more effort were made? God, there are so many examples. Here's one: Asians do up their homes with extravagant chandeliers and staircases to Buddha-knows-where, and then stick a fuck'n satellite dish the size of a campervan on their lawn. Or they stick a shitty TV on the wall of their shitty waiting area in their takeaway shops, and drape a fuck'n cable the length of the store to power it. They are such hard workers, so why, for the sake of half an hour, don't they pretty the place up? Question: Why can't Asians see cables?

PERSONALITY:

There is just not enough focus on it. Instead, people focus on academic qualifications, often at the expense of a good personality. We should produce more seers — broad of vision, with questioning minds and the ability to dream big. There are far too many closed-minded people leaving education with all the answers, not full of questions and a hunger and wonder to live. You can always learn facts — once you have lost the magic of dreams, it is gone forever!

KNOWING I AM RIGHT:

Just surrender yourself to the fact that I am. In all things, the views of Paul Henry are accurate. It took me several years to realise that my firmly-held views were spectacularly correct and required no second-guessing. Avoid doubt: this book is the new Bible!

CONCLUSION

I'm sorry, but were you not reading this book? It is a fuck'n outrage that I am expected to reach my own conclusion and do all the work for you. For Christ's sake, these are my fuck'n views. Come to your own conclusion! I already know that I am a wise sage with a core of genius, it's now time for you to realise it. Bugger, that's the conclusion. I have done it for you. Bugger.

This has not been cathartic at all, writing this damn book. I am as outraged as ever. Maybe more so. Fuck!

264

OMG - JUST BEEN TO THE
FEDERAL DELI FOR THE
FIRST TIME!
     FAN -TAS- TIC!
I DON'T NEED TO TWEET,
I'VE GOT A BOOK!

267

LAST PAGE

There is virtually no money in publishing in New Zealand for authors. Or, for that matter, for publishers, although they do tend to do better.

Most New Zealand authors struggle to pay for new biros! Having said that, most have greatly inflated opinions of their talents and are in fact crap!

I am a bestselling New Zealand author. Obviously. My first book, *What Was I Thinking*, in 2011, was a spectacular success, and yet it made me no more than a few tanks of gas for my boat. Mind you, it is a spectacularly big boat. I will be lucky to get even a thimble-full of diesel from the sale of this book you are holding now.

So why do it? My publisher said, 'Think of the publicity.' Well, try eating that!

COMPANION BOOK

Outraged is in a sense a companion book to *What Was I Thinking* by Paul Henry, published in 2011. As *Outraged* is a book of the opinions of Paul Henry, it is beneficial to the reader to get as much background on him as possible — the personal experiences and quirks that have shaped his views on life.

Obviously it is beneficial to Paul Henry that you purchase a copy of his other book. And you are encouraged here to do that as soon as you are able. If, like Paul, you have an obsessive-compulsive streak, you will not be able to live with an incomplete set! Regardless, to try to do so is foolhardy.

If you are one of the many who have already purchased a copy of Paul's first book: firstly, thank you. Secondly, consider the benefits of having another, new, pristine copy. Just for a moment, consider it . . . Exactly!

For more information about our titles visit
www.randomhouse.co.nz